English for MEETINGS

A2

SHORT COURSE SERIES

Dale Coulter

This book is also available online on
www.scook.de/eb

Please accept the terms and conditions to use the eBook.

Book Code: **vhtqc-363q3**

Impressum

Verfasser:	Dale Coulter
Berater:	Katherine Jähnig, Berlin
	Amy Sarow, Bielefeld
Projektleitung:	Andreas Göbel
Redaktion:	Anna Batrla, Meike Kolle
Außenredaktion:	Janan Barksdale, Berlin
Bildredaktion:	Janan Barksdale, Berlin
Redaktionelle Mitarbeit:	Oliver Busch, Christine House, Rani Kumar
Layoutkonzept:	finedesign, Berlin
Technische Umsetzung:	zweiband.media, Berlin
Umschlagsgestaltung:	Studio SYBERG, Berlin; Jan Haux / Pepe Jürgens, Berlin

Quellen

Titelfoto © Shutterstock, Leszek Glasner | **S. 4** v. o.: © Fotolia, BlueSkyImages; © Shutterstock, Monkey Business Images; © Shutterstock, Robert Kneschke; © Shutterstock, Blend Images; © Fotolia, Rido | **S. 5** v. o.: © Shutterstock, zhu difeng; © Shutterstock, Caroline Eibl; © Shutterstock, Monkey Business Images | **S. 6** v. o.: © Fotolia, BlueSkyImages; Shutterstock, VTT Studio | **S. 8** © Fotolia, Sergey Nivens | **S. 9** © Fotolia, Photographee.eu | **S. 11** © Fotolia, Rawpixel | **S. 12** © Shutterstock, Monkey Business Images | **S. 13** © Shutterstock, Stuart Jenner | **S. 15** © Fotolia, rogerphoto | **S. 17** © Fotolia, opolja | **S. 18** v. o.: © Shutterstock, Robert Kneschke – © Shutterstock, Epsicons (x6) | **S. 20** © Shutterstock, Dylanbz | **S. 21** © Shutterstock, LDprod | **S. 23** © Shutterstock, naihei | **S. 24** © Fotolia, Blend Images | **S. 25** © Shutterstock, Peter Nadolski | **S. 26** © Shutterstock, Goodluz | **S. 29** © Shutterstock, Andy Dean Photography | **S. 30** © Fotolia, Rido | **S. 31** © Shutterstock, Monkey Business Images | **S. 35** © Shutterstock, Dusit | **S. 36** © Shutterstock, zhu difeng | **S. 37** © Shutterstock, bikeriderlondon | **S. 38** v. l. © Shutterstock, wavebreakmedia – © Shutterstock, LDprod – © Shutterstock, Monkey Business Images – © Shutterstock, Stuart Jenner – © Shutterstock, LDprod | **S. 42** v. o.: © Shutterstock, Caroline Eibl – © Shutterstock, Maksin Schmeljov **S. 47** © Shutterstock, HomeStudio | **S. 48** © Shutterstock, Monkey Business Images | **S. 49** © Shutterstock, g-stockstudio | **S. 51** © Shutterstock, Monkey Business Images

www.cornelsen.de

1. Auflage, 1. Druck 2016

Alle Drucke dieser Auflage sind inhaltlich unverändert und können im Unterricht nebeneinander verwendet werden.

© 2016 Cornelsen Schulverlage GmbH, Berlin

Das Werk und seine Teile sind urheberrechtlich geschützt. Jede Nutzung in anderen als den gesetzlich zugelassenen Fällen bedarf der vorherigen schriftlichen Einwilligung des Verlages.

Hinweis zu den §§ 46, 52a UrhG: Weder das Werk noch seine Teile dürfen ohne eine solche Einwilligung eingescannt und in ein Netzwerk eingestellt oder sonst öffentlich zugänglich gemacht werden.

Dies gilt auch für Intranets von Schulen und sonstigen Bildungseinrichtungen.

Druck: Mohn Media Mohndruck, Gütersloh

ISBN 978-3-464-20573-0

PEFC zertifiziert
Dieses Produkt stammt aus nachhaltig bewirtschafteten Wäldern und kontrollierten Quellen.
www.pefc.de
PEFC/04-31-1033

English for Meetings im Überblick

Willkommen zu Ihrem A2 Short Course *English for Meetings*. Mit diesem Buch möchten wir Ihnen die sprachlichen Mittel und die Sicherheit vermitteln, um an englischsprachigen Geschäftsbesprechungen aktiv teilzunehmen. Wir schauen dafür auf unterschiedliche Geschäftssituationen, die Ihnen auch jederzeit im Ihrem beruflichen Alltag begegnen können. In acht Units entwickeln Sie die Fertigkeit und das notwendige Vokabular, um mit solch relevanten Themen wie bspw. die Tagesordnung durchgehen, Informationen klären oder die eigene Meinung wiedergeben umzugehen.

- Die acht Units erklären Schritt für Schritt an die grundlegende Formulierungen und das wichtigste Vokabular für Meetings.

- Im Buch spiegeln sich realistische Szenarien aus der Geschäftswelt wider, die Sie jederzeit auch in tatsächlichen Meetings antreffen werden. In vielfältigen Übungen haben Sie dann Gelegenheit, das Gelernte effektiv und nachhaltig umzusetzen.

- Die für Meetings wichtigsten Formulierungen eignen Sie sich aktiv mithilfe der *Phrase boxes* an und können diese am Ende jeder Unit noch einmal in den *Key phrases* wiederholen.

- Mit *Over to you* baut das Buch auf Ihren Kenntnissen im Bereich Geschäftsbesprechungen auf und fördert diese. Durch Partnerübungen werden Sie dazu animiert, miteinander zu kommunizieren.

- Jede Unit endet mit *Last but not least*, einem kurzen Text zum Thema, der ausgiebig zu Diskussionen einlädt.

- Authentische Dialoge auf der beiliegenden CD schulen Ihr Hörverstehen, damit Sie auch in den Meetings selbst jederzeit den Unterhaltungen mühelose folgen können. Eine Reihe von Akzenten bereitet Sie dabei auf diverse Geschäftspartner und Kollegen aus aller Welt vor.

- Im Anhang finden Sie eine umfassende Liste mit den wichtigsten Formulierungen. Auf diese können Sie jederzeit zurückgreifen, egal ob im Unterricht oder außerhalb. Zusätzlich gibt es dort die Transkripte für die Höraufgaben, einen Lösungsschlüssel und eine A-Z Wortliste.

Der Autor und die Redaktion wünschen Ihnen viel Freude mit *English for Meetings*! Wir hoffen, dass es Ihnen auf Ihrem Weg zu selbstbewussten Meetings auf Englisch einen gelungenen Beitrag leisten wird.

Inhaltsverzeichnis

1 Getting started

- Greeting someone
- Introducing yourself and others
- Making someone welcome
- Making small talk
- Starting a meeting

Page 6

I don't think we've met · shall we start? · welcome · I'd like to introduce · coffee and tea · small talk · take a seat · nice to meet you · flight

2 Beginning the meeting

- Describing your job or role
- Departments
- Talking about your experience
- Talking about the agenda

Page 12

I'm responsible for · department · experience · attendees · a copy of the agenda · years with the company · in charge of

3 Giving updates

- Asking for an update
- Giving an update
- Checking understanding
- Accepting tasks

Page 18

on schedule · at the moment · what's the news? · do you mean? · I'll take care of it · deadlines · did you say? · no problem

4 Taking part in a discussion

- Giving your opinion
- Making a suggestion
- Agreeing
- Disagreeing

Page 24

we should · in my opinion · I think that · looks good · why don't we? · good idea · I'm afraid I don't agree · I see what you mean

5 Problems and solutions

- Describing a problem
- Looking for a solution
- Offering a solution
- Delaying making a decision

Page 30

what can we do? · missing deadlines · wait until tomorrow · next week · unfortunately · let's discuss · any other ideas?

6 Conference calls

- Entering a call and getting started
- Dealing with problems
- Clarifying information

> problems with the line
> can you hear me? did you say?
> just to be clear log in ready to begin
> who's speaking? volume
> in other words sorry

Page 36

7 Arranging a meeting

- Arranging a meeting
- Saying you can or can't attend
- Rearranging a meeting
- Confirming a meeting

> could we meet? let us know
> tomorrow instead
> sorry I'm calling to confirm
> sounds good can't make it
> at 2:15 p.m.

Page 42

8 Leading a meeting

- Introducing the agenda
- Asking for feedback
- Checking the time
- Delegating tasks
- Summarizing and closing a meeting

> do you agree?
> action points take the minutes
> after that, we'll agenda items
> chairperson see you next time
> to summarize thanks for coming

Page 48

Anhang

Page 54 Transcripts
Page 56 Answer key
Page 60 Phrases (English–German)
Page 68 A–Z wordlist
Page 72 Tracklist

Symbole und Abkürzungen

◁) 02 Tracknummer
　　　Partnerarbeit
AE　amerikanisches Englisch
BE　britisches Englisch
sb.　somebody (jemand)
sth.　something (etwas)

1 Getting started

Learning objectives
- Greeting someone
  Jemanden begrüßen
- Introducing yourself and others
  Sich und andere vorstellen
- Starting a meeting
  Ein Meeting eröffnen

1 Read these short dialogues. Which can you use with …

a someone you know? .... b someone you don't know? ....

1
- It's a pleasure to meet you.
- It's nice to meet you too.

2
- It's nice to see you again!
- Good to see you too.

3
- I don't think we've met. My name is Jan Golz.
- Pleased to meet you, Jan. I'm Anne Baker.

Who do you normally have meetings with? People you know or people you meet for the first time? Tell a partner.

2 ◁) 02 Read and listen to the dialogue. How well does Susanne know Magda? Tick (✓) the topics they talk about.

☐ the trip   ☐ family   ☐ the weather   ☐ vacations

Vocabulary
flight Flug
to take a seat Platz nehmen
vacation Urlaub

Susanne Good morning. You must be Ms. Kowalski. I'm Susanne Müller.
Magda   Good morning. It's a pleasure to meet you. Please call me Magda.
Susanne And I'm Susanne. It's nice to meet you too. Did you find us OK?
Magda   Yes, thank you. I took a taxi from the airport.
Susanne Very good. And how was your flight?
Magda   Fine, thanks.
Susanne Super. Well, here we are. Can I take your coat?
Magda   Yes, thank you. It's so warm today, I didn't really need a coat.
Susanne Yes, it is really nice. What's the weather like in Warsaw?
Magda   It's still cool, but it was nice and sunny this morning.
Susanne So, please take a seat. Would you like some coffee?
Magda   Yes, please.
Susanne Here you are. And here's milk and sugar.
         So, let's get started. Thank you for coming. …

How was your flight? (not *How was your fly?*)

English for Meetings

3 🔊 03 Now read and listen to this dialogue. Which two participants already know each other?

☐ Rob and Anja
☐ Rob and Lina
☐ Anja and Lina

Vocabulary

agenda Tagesordnung
to be responsible sth. für etw. zuständig sein
to join a team neu in ein Team kommen
participant Teilnehmer/in
representative Vertreter/in

Rob   Hi, Anja.
Anja Good afternoon, Rob. Nice to see you again. How are things?
Rob   Good thanks, and with you?
Anja Not bad. Oh, this is my colleague, Lina Pohl. I don't think you've met. Lina has just joined the team and will be responsible for our Scandinavian project. Lina, Rob here is the representative from our UK partner, Intaco.
Lina It's nice to meet you, Rob.
Rob   You too.
Anja Well, I think we should get started. Did you both get a copy of the agenda for today? …

4 Look at the dialogues in exercises 2 and 3 again and complete the phrases below.

Phrases

Greeting someone

Good morning. You ....¹ Ms. Kowalski.

It's ....² to meet you.

It's ....³ you too.

Good afternoon, Rob. Nice to ....⁴. How are things?

Good thanks, ...⁵ you?

Introducing yourself and others

..................⁶ Susanne Müller.

Please ....⁷ Magda.

This ....⁸, Lina Pohl. I don't think you've met.

Making someone welcome

So, ...⁹ a seat. Would ....¹⁰ some coffee?

> It's nice to meet you.
> = Schön, Sie kennenzulernen.
> It's nice to see you (again).
> = Schön, Sie (wieder)zusehen.

> **Did you know?**
> "So" and "well" are often used to change the subject in a conversation.
> So, please take a seat.
> Well, I think we should get started.

5 Match the two parts of these sentences.

1 Nice to   a colleague, Paul Lenz.
2 How   b you've met.
3 This is my   c call me Hanna.
4 I don't think   d see you again.
5 Please take a seat e are things?
6 And please   f and have some coffee if you'd like.

6 🔊 04 **Listen to three short dialogues and tick the phrases you hear.**

Dialogue 1

1 a ☐ Nice to see you.
  b ☐ Nice to see you again.

2 a ☐ How are things?
  b ☐ How are you?

Dialogue 2

3 a ☐ It's nice to finally meet you.
  b ☐ Pleased to meet you.

4 a ☐ Please call me Javier.
  b ☐ And I'm Javier.

Dialogue 3

5 a ☐ Good afternoon, everyone.
  b ☐ Hi, everyone.

6 a ☐ Please have some coffee if you'd like.
  b ☐ Please take a seat.

Vocabulary
documents Unterlagen
to forget vergessen
to introduce sb. jdn. vorstellen
to look forward to sich auf etw. freuen

7 **Complete the dialogue with the phrases below.**

> How are things? • It's a pleasure to meet you. • It's nice to see you both again. •
> Would anyone like some coffee? • So, let's get started. • This is Natascha Eder.

Anton   Good afternoon, Angela. Afternoon, Thomas. .... ¹

Angela   You too, Anton. .... ²

Anton   Good, thanks. Before we get started, I'd like to introduce a new colleague. ....
           .... ³ She's responsible for the team in Austria.

Natascha   .... ⁴ I look forward to working with you.

Thomas/Angela   Me too.

Anton   .... ⁵ Did you all get the documents I sent last week?

All   Yes. / Yes, I have them here.

Anton   Great. Oh, and before I forget: .... ⁶

8 **Match the sentences and phrases which mean the same thing.**

1 How are things?
2 It's a pleasure to meet you.
3 Let's get started.
4 I'd like to introduce …
5 And I'm …
6 It's nice to see you again.

a Shall we start?
b This is …
c Please call me …
d It's nice to meet you.
e Great to see you.
f How are you?

9 🔊 05 Read and listen to this dialogue. Who will be late for the meeting?

Paul	Hi everyone, good to see you all. Is Andreas on his way?
Marit	Yes, he'll be here in a minute.
Paul	OK. And has anyone seen Julia today?
Lars/Marit	No, I haven't. / No.
Christian	Oh, sorry, I forgot to say. She's not here today. She's not feeling well.
Paul	OK, thanks. Well, shall we start? Does everyone have a copy of the agenda for today? Yes? Good.

Vocabulary

late (zu) spät
to not feel well krank sein
on his / her way auf dem Weg, unterwegs

10 Look at the dialogue in exercise 9 again and complete the phrases below.

> **Phrases**
>
> **Starting a meeting**
>
> Hi everyone, ……………………………¹ all.
>
> Well, shall we start?
>
> Does ……………………………² a copy of the agenda for today?
>
> **Talking about participants**
>
> Andreas is on his way. He'll be here in a minute.
>
> And ……………………………³ Julia today?
>
> She's not here today. She's not ……………………………⁴.

11 Put the words into the correct order to make questions.

1 on | Is | his | Peter | way   *Is Peter on his way* ?
2 today | anyone | Has | Anna | seen …………………………… ?
3 the | Does | have | agenda | everyone …………………………… ?
4 anyone | Would | tea or coffee | like | some …………………………… ?
5 get | we | started | Shall …………………………… ?

Now match the questions to the answers.

☐ a Oh, no, sorry. I forgot my copy.
1 b Yes, he's in another meeting, but he'll be here in a minute.
☐ c Can we wait for Ralf? He'll be here in a minute.
☐ d No, thanks.
☐ e No, but she called earlier. She's not feeling well today.

Unit 1 . Getting started   9

Key phrases

Here are some key phrases from the unit. Tick the ones that are useful for you.

Greeting someone you don't know
- You must be Ms. Kowalski.
- It's a pleasure to (finally) meet you.
- It's nice to meet you (too).
- Pleased to meet you.
- I look forward to working with you.

Greeting someone you know
- It's nice / Nice to see you (again).
- Good to see you too.
- How are you? – I'm well / Not bad, thanks.
- How are things? – Good, thanks. And with you?

Introducing others
- I'd like to introduce a new colleague. She's responsible for …
- This is (my colleague) Maria Lopez.
- I don't think you've met.

Introducing yourself
- I'm Anna Schmidt, but please call me Anna. – And I'm David.
- I don't think we've met. My name is Jan Golz.

Making someone welcome
- Can I take your coat? – Thank you.
- Please take a seat and have some coffee / tea / water if you'd like.
- Would you like some coffee?

Talking about participants
- Is Andreas on his way? – Yes, he'll be here in a minute.
- And has anyone seen Julia? – She's not here today. She's not feeling well.

Getting started

Starting a meeting
- Well, shall we start?
- So, let's get started.
- Good morning / Good afternoon / Hi (everyone).
- It's good to see you all.
- Thank you (all) for coming.
- Did everyone get / Does everyone have a a copy of the agenda?

Making small talk
- Is this your first time in Frankfurt? – No, I was here last year, so I know the city a little. / Yes, it is. But I've wanted to come for a while.
- Did you find us OK? – Yes, thank you.
- How was your flight / trip / train ride? – Fine, thanks.

You will find an English-German list of these phrases on pages 60–61.

Use this space to write your own useful words and phrases.

....
....
....
....
....

Over to you

12 What phrases could you use before a meeting? Write down how you would do the following.

Greet someone you know: ....

Greet someone you don't know and introduce yourself: ....

....

Introduce someone: ....

....

Now work with two partners and practice the dialogue. When you finish, change roles and do the activity again.

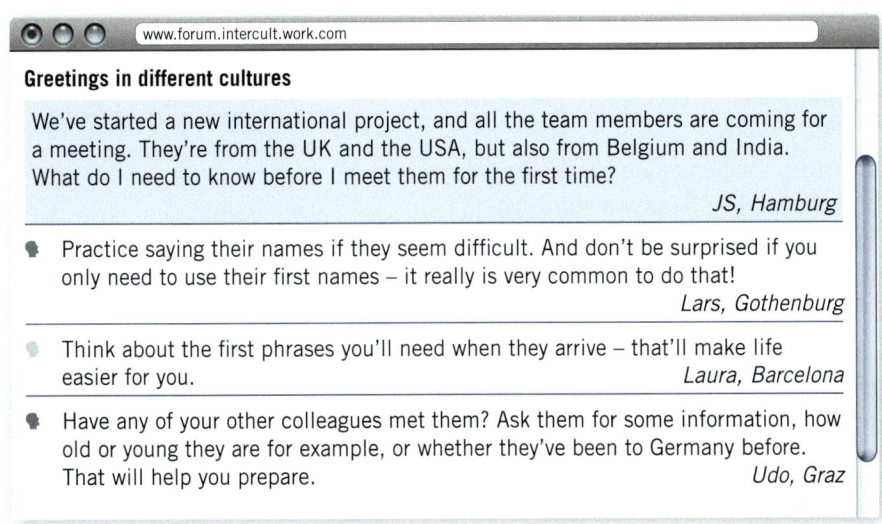

A Greet someone you don't know and introduce yourself.

B Reply.

A Introduce B to C.

B Reply and introduce yourself.

A Ask B about his / her trip.

B **C** Reply and make small talk.

A Reply and start the meeting.

B **C** Reply.

A Ask B and C to sit down and offer drinks.

Last but not least

13 Have a look at this online forum. Have you experienced something similar? What do you think of the advice?

Vocabulary

advice Ratschlag, Ratschläge
common gängig
to prepare sich vorbereiten
similar ähnlich
surprised überrascht

www.forum.intercult.work.com

Greetings in different cultures

We've started a new international project, and all the team members are coming for a meeting. They're from the UK and the USA, but also from Belgium and India. What do I need to know before I meet them for the first time?

JS, Hamburg

- Practice saying their names if they seem difficult. And don't be surprised if you only need to use their first names – it really is very common to do that!

Lars, Gothenburg

- Think about the first phrases you'll need when they arrive – that'll make life easier for you.

Laura, Barcelona

- Have any of your other colleagues met them? Ask them for some information, how old or young they are for example, or whether they've been to Germany before. That will help you prepare.

Udo, Graz

How do you prepare when you have to meet new people at work? What advice can you give? Discuss with a partner.

2 Beginning the meeting

1 Match the types of meetings (1–4) to the descriptions (a–d).

1 ☐ departmental meeting
2 ☐ teleconference (meeting)
3 ☐ one-on-one meeting
4 ☐ kick-off meeting

a meeting on the phone
b meeting with just two people
c the first meeting for a project
d meeting of people in one part of a company, e.g. marketing

Vocabulary

to attend teilnehmen
instead stattdessen
to take place stattfinden

Tick the meetings you attend regularly. How often do they take place (once a week, twice a month, etc.)?

Did you know?

The term "Jour fixe" is not used to describe meetings in English. Use "weekly meeting" or "regular meeting" instead.

2 ◁ 06 Read and listen to the beginning of a meeting. What kind of meeting is it? Do the participants all work in the same company?

Sabine Hello, everyone. Great to see you. Shall we get started? As this is the first meeting for this project, let's start by introducing ourselves and saying a bit about our role here or in the company. Marcus, would you like to start?

Marcus Sure. I'm Marcus Bering. I've been with the company for about ten years. I work in the finance department and I'll be in charge of the budget – making sure we don't spend too much.

Sabine Thanks, Marcus. That's an important job. Louise, do you want to continue? And then go around the room?

Louise OK. Well, I'm Louise. I'm from Chicago but I moved here from our office in the States two years ago. I still work closely with the team there, selling our products worldwide.

Mae My name is Mae Chen. I work in the IT department and will be responsible for the team who will do the programming. I've worked on similar projects for other departments and am looking forward to this one.

Tom And I'm Tom Haas. I just moved here from another company, and also another country – the Netherlands. I'm head of customer relations, so my job is to make sure our clients are happy.

Sabine Thanks everyone, that's great. And now it's my turn. I'm part of the research and development department, and I'm leading this project. So, let's look at the …

Vocabulary

to be in charge of sth.
  für etw. zuständig sein
department Abteilung
head Leiter/in
to lead leiten
to move umziehen
to spend (Geld) ausgeben

3 Look at the dialogue again and complete the phrases below.

> I've been with the company for ten years.
> (not I am with the company since ten years.)

Phrases

Talking about your experience

I've ....¹ the company for about ten years …

I moved here from our office in the States ....².

I've worked ....³ for other departments.

..............................⁴ here from another company …

Describing your job / role

I ....⁵ the finance department and I'll be ....⁶ the budget …

I still ....⁷ with the team there …

I work in the IT department and ....⁸ for the team who will do the programming.

..............................⁹ customer relations, so my job is to make sure our clients are happy.

I'm ....¹⁰ research and development department, and I'm ....¹¹ this project.

4 Complete the sentences with the words in the box.

for · in · of · on · to · with · with

1 I work closely .... the sales team.
2 I work .... the finance department.
3 I've worked .... other IT projects before.
4 I've been .... the company .... four years.
5 I'm part .... the marketing department.
6 I'm looking forward .... this project.

5 Match these department names to the German equivalent.

1 production
2 finance
3 human resources (HR)
4 sales
5 customer relations
6 research and development (R&D)

a Kundenservice
b Finanzabteilung
c Vertrieb
d Herstellung
e Forschung und Entwicklung
f Personalabteilung

What other departments does your company have? Compare answers with a partner.

6 🔊 07 Read and listen to these short dialogues.

1. A Good morning. Come in, have a seat. Is everyone here?
   B Um, Hans is on his way. He should be here in a minute.
   C Joscha will also be late.
   A OK, well let's wait for them to arrive before we get started.

2. A Afternoon, sorry I'm late. I was on the phone.
   B No problem, Jim. Gabi is just updating us on the Interco project.
   C Ah, yes, as I was saying, we're …

3. A Good afternoon. Nice to see you again. Please come in and take a seat. And please have some tea or coffee if you'd like. We'll start in a minute or so when Michael Thiel arrives. In the meantime, here is a copy of the agenda.
   B, C, D Thank you. / Thanks.

> **Vocabulary**
> in the meantime in der Zwischenzeit
> to update auf den neuesten Stand bringen

> Sorry I'm *late*.
> (not ~~Sorry I'm too late.~~)

Are the statements below true or false?

	True	False
1 Hans and Joscha are both late for the meeting.	☐	☐
2 Gabi is giving an update on the Interco project.	☐	☐
3 Meeting 3 takes place in the morning.	☐	☐
4 Mr. Thiel is already at the meeting.	☐	☐

7 Now look at the agenda for meeting 3 and answer the questions opposite.

> **Vocabulary**
> agenda item Tagesordnungspunkt
> apologies entschuldigt
> attendee Teilnehmer/in
> minutes Protokoll

Agenda

Update meeting
Thursday, June 4, 20.., 3–4.15 p.m.
Conference room (2.033)

Attendees: *Arne Jacobsen, Paul Janssen, Francesca Paolini, Laura Smith, Michael Thiel*
Special guests: *Hilda Jensen, Allan Juhl and Anne-Mette Guldhammer from Dan-Design*

Agenda Items	Who	Time (mins)
1 Welcome and apologies	Michael	2
2 Minutes from meeting of April 2	Arne	5
3 Update		
- budget	Francesca	10
- problems with computer system	Laura	5
4 Update (Dan-Design)		
- changes within team	Hilda	10
5 Next steps and date for next meeting	Michael	10
6 Misc.		10

> Sonstiges
> Misc. (miscellaneous)   AOB (any other business)
> American English   British English

14 English for Meetings

1 When and where does the meeting take place? ....
2 How many people are attending the meeting? ....
3 Why are they having the meeting? ....
4 How many items are on the agenda? ....

8 ◁08 Read how meeting 3 continues and complete the dialogue with the words below. Then listen and check.

agenda · budget · items · late · started · updates

Laura	Ah, here's Michael now.
Michael	Yes, sorry I'm ....¹. Thank you for waiting, and thank you all for coming. So, let's get ....². Shall we go through the ....³ first?
Attendees	Yes. / OK.
Michael	Excellent. Arne, can you take the minutes today?
Arne	Of course.
Michael	Thanks. So, the main ....⁴ on the agenda are ....⁵ from both of our teams: from our team, on the ....⁶ and the problems we're having with our computer system, and from Dan-Design, …
Hilda	Sorry, Michael. Could you also update us on the changes in your company?
Michael	That's a good point. I can say a few words about that. Let me just add that to the agenda, before the budget, OK? … Are there any other points we should add?
Laura	Yes, I have a point for miscellaneous. I think we need to discuss …

Vocabulary

to add hinzufügen
to go through durchgehen
to take the minutes
 Protokoll führen

9 Look at the dialogue again and complete the phrases below.

> **Phrases**
>
> **Talking about the agenda**
>
> In the meantime, here is a copy of the agenda.
>
> Shall we ....¹ first?
>
> Arne, can you ....² today?
>
> The ....³ the agenda are …
>
> Are there ....⁴ we should add?

10 Think of a meeting you attended recently and tell a partner …

- who attended the meeting.
- how many items were on the agenda.
- if anyone added points to the agenda after the meeting started.
- who took the minutes.

Key phrases

Here are some key phrases from the unit. Tick the ones that are useful for you.

You will find an English–German list of these phrases on pages 61–62.

Beginning the meeting

Describing your job or role
- ☐ I work in the … department and I'll be in charge of …
- ☐ I work closely with the team here / there / in Poland.
- ☐ I'm head of …
- ☐ I'm part of the … department.
- ☐ I am / will be responsible for …
- ☐ I'm leading this project.

Departments
accounting
customer relations
finance
HR (human resources)
IT (information technology)
marketing
production
purchasing
quality control
R&D (research and development)
sales

Talking about your experience
- ☐ I've been with the company for about ten years.
- ☐ I moved here from our Chicago office two years ago.
- ☐ I just moved here from production / another company.
- ☐ I've worked on similar projects for other departments.

Talking about the agenda
- ☐ Here is a copy of the agenda.
- ☐ Shall we go through the agenda first?
- ☐ The main items on the agenda are …
- ☐ Are there any other points we should add?
- ☐ Can you take the minutes today?

Types of meetings
- one-on-one meeting
- ....
- departmental meeting
- kick-off meeting
- teleconference (meeting)

Use this space to write your own useful words and phrases.

....
....
....
....
....

English for Meetings

Over to you

11 Think of the meetings you attend with people who don't know you. Write down how you would do the following:

Introduce yourself: ....

Describe your job or role: ....

....

Talk about your experience: ....

....

Now work with a partner and practice the dialogue. When you finish, change roles and do the activity again.

A Start the meeting by welcoming attendees and introducing yourself.

B Introduce yourself and talk about your experience.

A Talk about the agenda.

Last but not least

12 Gabi is part of a new project team and doesn't know how to introduce herself at the first meeting. She asks her colleague Marcus for some advice. Do you agree with what he writes?

Subject: *Re: How do I introduce myself at a meeting?*

Dear Gabi,

Good question. When you introduce yourself, I think it's best to use a few key questions to help you.

– Who are you?
– What do you do?
– What is your role in the project?
– Why are you at the meeting?

Think about these four questions when you are talking. They will help you to focus on what is important and to keep your introduction short.

Also, if you know you're the only non-native speaker of English at the meeting, perhaps speak to the person leading the meeting before and explain this. It can be useful for him/her to know that your level of English is low.

I hope this helps.

Marcus

Vocabulary

to agree with sth. mit etw. übereinstimmen
to keep sth. short etw. kurz halten
low niedrig

Have you ever been in a similar situation?
What would you say to Gabi? Discuss with your partner and add any other tips you have.

Learning objectives
- Asking for and giving an update
  Ein Update einfordern und geben
- Checking understanding and accepting tasks
  Rückfragen stellen und Aufgaben annehmen

3 Giving updates

1. Put the tasks below in order of importance for your job (1 = most important, 6 = least important). Which tasks do you sometimes talk about when giving an update? Compare your answers with a partner.

   ☐ Send emails   ☐ Write a report   ☐ Meet a client for lunch
   ☐ Give a presentation   ☐ Visit a factory   ☐ Write a budget plan

2. ♪09 Read and listen to the dialogues. In which dialogue(s) is there a problem?

   ☐ Dialogue 1   ☐ Dialogue 2   ☐ Dialogue 3

1
Alexander: One more thing. What's the news on the stand for the trade fair?
Paula: Well, we finished the design concept. At the moment we're building the stand and everything's on schedule.
Alexander: So we'll meet the deadline. Great.

2
Klara: How is the monthly newsletter going?
Jon: We're still waiting for an update from our supplier. I emailed them, but they haven't answered yet. I'm going to call them after the meeting.
Klara: Sounds good.

3
Uwe: So the next thing is the sales conference. Can you give me an update on that?
Jeremy: Um, yes. We're visiting some new venues this week.
Uwe: Wait, I thought we already had a venue. What happened?
Jeremy: I'm afraid the hotel cancelled the reservation, so we had to look for a new one.
Uwe: Oh no, that's bad news.
Jeremy: Don't worry. I've made a list of five alternatives. Here, have a look.

Vocabulary
to be on schedule im Zeitplan liegen
I'm afraid leider
to meet the deadline den Termin einhalten
supplier Lieferant
trade fair Messe
venue Veranstaltungsort

not … yet = noch nicht

3 Look at the dialogues in exercise 2 again and complete the phrases below.

Phrases

Asking for an update

_____¹ the stand for the trade fair?

_____² the monthly newsletter going?

So the next thing is the sales conference. Can you _____³ that?

Giving an update

Well, _____⁴ the design concept.

At _____⁵ we're building the stand and everything's _____⁶.

We're _____⁷ an update from our supplier.

I emailed them, but they _____⁸.

_____⁹ some new venues this week.

4 Match the two parts of the phrases below.

1 Can you give us   on schedule.
2 How is   an update on …?
3 … it should be here   ordered it …
4 Everything's   anyone yet.
5 We haven't found   that going?
6 We've already   news …?
7 What's the   next week.

Which phrases are used to …

a ask for an update? _____

b give an update? _____

Vocabulary

delivery Lieferung
furniture Möbel
search (for sb.) Suche (nach jdm.)
That's too bad. Schade.

5 Now use the phrases in exercise 4 to complete the dialogue below.

A _____¹ on the office furniture?

B _____² but we're still waiting for delivery. I spoke with the supplier and they said that _____³.

A Good. The next point is the search for the new assistant. _____⁴?

C Not so well, I'm afraid. _____⁵.

A That's too bad. OK. So, last point. _____⁶ the new project, Peter?

D Yes, I can. _____⁷.

6 🔊 10 Read and listen to the dialogues. Tick the items on the to-do list that Jana and her colleagues discuss. Which task does she delegate to a colleague?

1

Gregor	How are you doing with the reports? We need them by Thursday at the latest.
Jana	I'm working on them, but … . Sorry, did you say Tuesday or Thursday?
Gregor	Thursday.
Jana	Good. I can do that, no problem.

2

Jana	So there will be 14 of us at the meeting, right?
Robert	Yes, that's right. I think we should book room 218.
Jana	Sorry, was that 218 or 318?
Robert	218.
Jana	OK, I'll book the room. And you'll check the technical equipment, right?
Robert	Yes, I'll take care of that.

3

Rani	The next thing is the contract for the Comstat meeting. Could you please print out six copies?
Jana	Do you mean six copies of the whole contract?
Rani	Actually, just the first five pages. The rest is standard, and they only have to check their details.
Jana	Fine, just the first five pages then. I'll do that right away.

To-do list

check technical equipment ☐
book conference room ☐
finish reports ☐
email attendees ☐
print contracts ☐

by + deadline:
I need the reports by Thursday.
(not ~~until Thursday~~)

Vocabulary

at the latest   spätestens
contract   Vertrag
to delegate   delegieren
right away   sofort
to take care of   sich kümmern um

I'll do that right away.
(not ~~I do that~~)

7 Look at the dialogues in exercise 6 again and complete the phrases below.

Phrases

Checking understanding

Sorry, ...¹ Tuesday or Thursday?

So there will be 14 of us at the meeting, ...²?

Sorry, ...³ 218 or 318?

........................⁴ six copies of the whole contract?

Accepting tasks

I ....⁵, no problem.

Yes, I'll ....⁶ that.

........................⁷, just the first five pages then. I'll ....⁸.

Did you know?

"Yes, that's right" or "Yes, no problem" is more polite than just "Yes".
It's also more natural to say "I'm afraid I can't" or "No, sorry" than just "No".

8 Use words from the box to complete the dialogues.

> actually · afraid · by · mean · right · right away · take care · was

1 A Could you give Anna a quick call and check the progress?

   B Sorry, do you ....¹ Anna or Anne?

   A Oh, sorry. Anne, of course.

   B Sure. I'll call her ....².

2 A Could you let the customer know about the two changes to the order?

   B ....³, I think there were three changes. Can you check?

   A Yes, you're right. Three changes. Can you let them know?

   B Yes, I can .... ⁴ of that.

3 A The good news is that the supplier delivered 30 out of 40 orders on time.

   B Sorry, ...⁵ that 13 or 30?

   A Thirty. And the order for Poland should arrive next week.

   B That's the large order, ...⁶? Can you give me the details?

   A I'm ....⁷ I can't right now, but I'll let you know ....⁸ this afternoon.

Vocabulary

to let sb. know jdm. Bescheid geben
on time pünktlich, rechtzeitig
order Bestellung, Auftrag
progress Fortschritt(e)

Did you know?

You can use "actually" to correct someone politely.
Actually, her name is Sue, not Susan.

9 You and a colleague are meeting to discuss and delegate tasks. Work with a partner to make mini-dialogues using the prompts below. Take turns checking understanding, explaining, and accepting the task (or not).

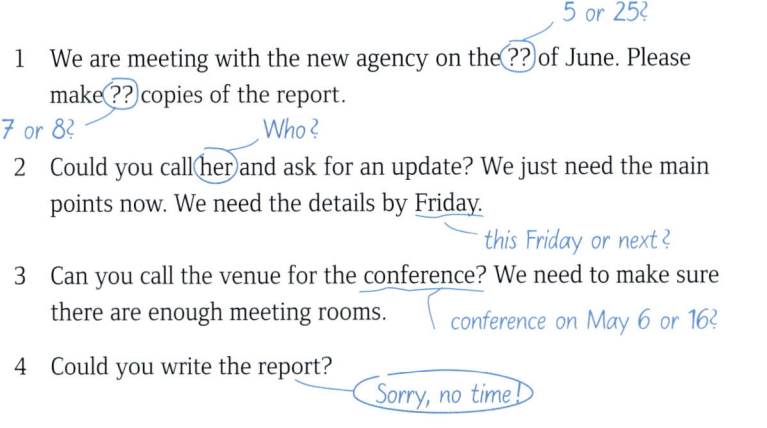

1 We are meeting with the new agency on the ?? of June. Please make ?? copies of the report. *(5 or 25?)* *(7 or 8?)*

2 Could you call her and ask for an update? We just need the main points now. We need the details by Friday. *(Who?)* *(this Friday or next?)*

3 Can you call the venue for the conference? We need to make sure there are enough meeting rooms. *(conference on May 6 or 16?)*

4 Could you write the report? *(Sorry, no time!)*

Sorry, was that the fifth or the twenty-fifth?

Now make your own dialogue to practice delegating tasks and checking understanding.

Key phrases

Here are some key phrases from the unit. Tick the ones that are useful for you.

Asking for an update
- [ ] What's the news on …?
- [ ] Is there any news on …?
- [ ] How is the project going?
- [ ] Can you give me/us an update?
- [ ] How are you doing with …?

Giving an update
- [ ] We finished the …
- [ ] We've already ordered/done …
- [ ] We haven't done … yet.
- [ ] We're still waiting for …
- [ ] We're visiting some new venues this week.
- [ ] At the moment, we're building/visiting …
- [ ] We're on schedule.
- [ ] So we'll meet the deadline.

Giving updates

Accepting tasks (or not)
- [ ] I can do that, no problem.
- [ ] Fine. I'll do it/that right away.
- [ ] I can / I'll take care of that.
- [ ] Sorry, I'm afraid I can't right now.

Checking understanding
- [ ] Sorry, was that … or …?
- [ ] Sorry, but did you say Tuesday or Thursday?
- [ ] So there will be …, right?
- [ ] Do you mean …?

You will find an English–German list of these phrases on page 63.

Use this space to write your own useful words and phrases.

....
....
....
....
....
....
....
....
....

Over to you

10 What tasks do you normally have at work? Make a list.

Tasks:

....

....

....

11 You are going on vacation for two weeks and your partner is going to do your job while you are away. Give him/her an update on the project and explain what to do. Then change roles.

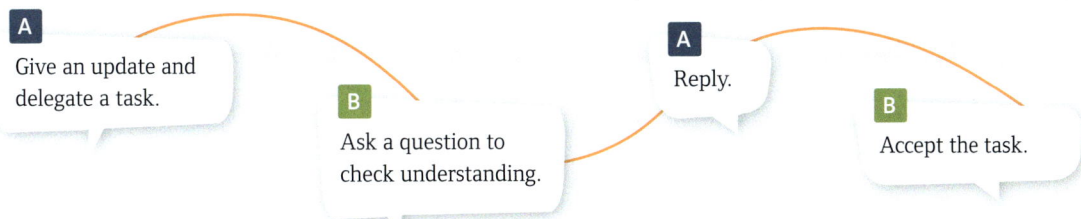

A Give an update and delegate a task.

B Ask a question to check understanding.

A Reply.

B Accept the task.

Last but not least

Vocabulary

disorganized   unorganisiert
to fly by   vorüberfliegen
to improve   verbessern
wooshing sound   Rauschen, Zischen

12 Read these statements on deadlines and time management. Number them (1–4) in order of how relevant they are to your work, then compare with a partner.

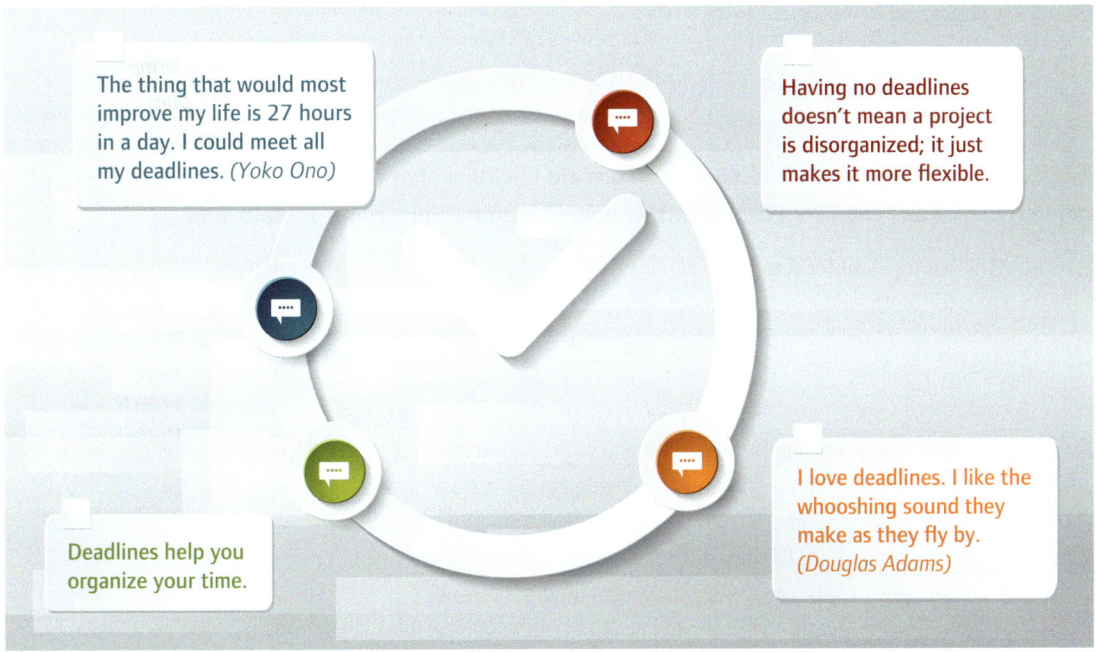

The thing that would most improve my life is 27 hours in a day. I could meet all my deadlines. *(Yoko Ono)*

Having no deadlines doesn't mean a project is disorganized; it just makes it more flexible.

Deadlines help you organize your time.

I love deadlines. I like the whooshing sound they make as they fly by. *(Douglas Adams)*

4 Taking part in a discussion

Learning objectives
- Giving your opinion
  Die eigene Meinung wiedergeben
- Making a suggestion
  Einen Vorschlag machen
- Agreeing and disagreeing
  Zustimmen und widersprechen

1 Read these different attitudes on giving your opinion. Which do you agree with the most? Which do you agree with the least? Discuss with your partner.

> 1 I think it's important to have everyone's opinion, even if you disagree with them.

> 3 In my opinion, there should always be someone who disagrees. If everybody agrees all the time, nothing gets better.

> 2 I guess it is OK to say negative things, but it's important to say them politely.

> 4 It's important not to disagree too much.

2 ◁) 11 Janina and her colleagues Kyle and Carlos are having a planning meeting about the launch of a new product. Read and listen to the extract below. Janina thinks it is a good idea to …

- [ ] move the launch date to March.
- [ ] start the launch later.
- [ ] make a new timeline.

Vocabulary

delay Verzögerung
launch Markteinführung
to move verschieben
to suggest vorschlagen
timeline Zeitplan

Kyle	Do you think we will be ready for the launch in March?
Janina	Hmm. In my opinion, March is a little early. We are still waiting for too many things.
Carlos	Oh, that's too bad. What do you suggest?
Janina	Personally, I think we should move the launch to June.
Kyle	June? Are you sure? That means it will take three more months!
Carlos	Can I say something here? In my experience, delays are quite common. I don't think that will be a problem.
Kyle	OK, good. Then let's change the launch date to June 1st.

24   English for Meetings

3 🔊 12 Now read and listen to two extracts from a different meeting, this time between Phil, a structural engineer, his boss and a consultant. What do they agree to do?

1 .... 2 ....

Vocabulary

consultant Berater/in
to reduce costs Kosten senken
structural engineer Bauingenieur/in
to supply bereitstellen

1 Boss   In my opinion, supplying parking for 30 cars will be difficult in this area of the city.
   Phil   Good point. What about putting half the parking under the building?
   Boss   Sure, that sounds like a good idea. …

2 Boss   What do you think about the timeline? I think it looks quite good.
   Phil   Yes, I think so too. It's smart to do the construction work in the summer.
   Consultant Yes, I agree. It will reduce costs, and make everything go more quickly.

4 Look at the dialogues in exercise 2 and 3 again and complete the phrases below.

Phrases

Giving your opinion

In ....¹, March is a little early.

In ....², delays are quite common.

I ....³ that will be a problem.

Agreeing with someone

Good point.

Sure, that ....⁴ a good idea.

Yes, I ....⁵ too.

Yes, I ....⁶. It will reduce costs …

Making a suggestion

Personally, I ....⁷ move the launch to June.

....⁸ half the parking under the building?

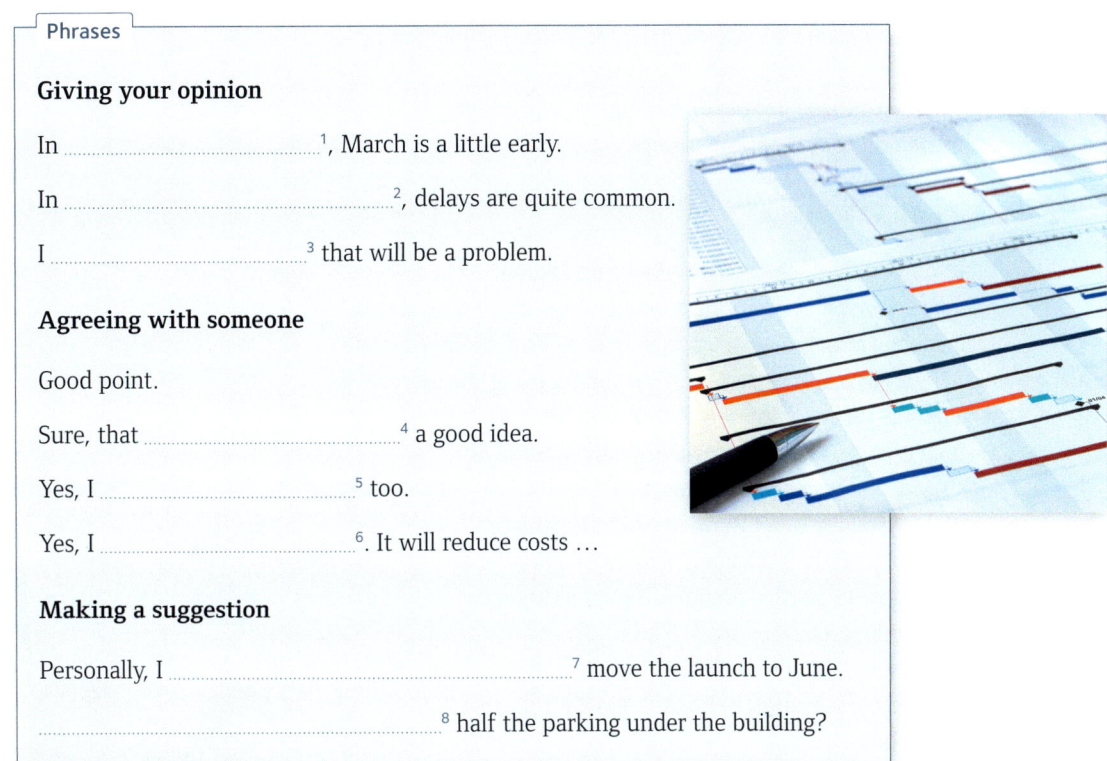

5 Match the two parts of these sentences.

1 I think 30 minutes   a so too.
2 I agree   b advertising online?
3 In my experience,   c delivery usually takes two weeks.
4 What about   d like a good idea.
5 That sounds   e is enough for the presentation.
6 I think   f with Paul's suggestion.

6 Put the words in the correct order to complete these opinions and suggestions. There is one word you don't need in each phrase.

1 (my | offer | in | opinion) ...., it's not a good idea to travel to Rome for the meeting. It's just too expensive. Are there any alternatives?

2 I don't think that sales will be that high. However, there's a good way to find out.
(don't | why | check | we | not) .... with the sales team?

3 Just so you know, (think | I | we | thinking | have) .... enough material for three newsletters.

4 (speaking | when | about | what) .... to your manager about the problem?

Now match them to these replies.
a ☐ Good, so why don't we prepare all three now?
b ☐ What about having a teleconference? Then nobody has to travel anywhere.
c ☐ Good point. I'll talk to them at our next meeting.
d ☐ That sounds like a good idea. I'll ask her later if she has time for a chat.

7 🔊 13 Read and listen to three people discussing new product packaging. Choose one of the options below.

☐ Karl disagrees with Julia   ☐ Julia disagrees with Stuart

Vocabulary
cheap günstig
expensive teuer
packaging Verpackung

Julia	What do you think of the first type of packaging?
Stuart	It looks very creative, very high quality. How much does it cost?
Julia	Well, it's the most expensive option, but that's not important.
Stuart	Actually, I think it is important. What about using cheaper material? Is that an option? What do you think, Karl?
Karl	I see your point, Stuart, but we want the product to look good, and packaging is important.
Stuart	Hmm. I personally don't think we should spend too much money on the packaging. Expensive packaging means a more expensive product. We should spend money on the product instead.
Julia	Well, I'm afraid I don't agree. Karl is right – the packaging is important too. But let's look at the second option …

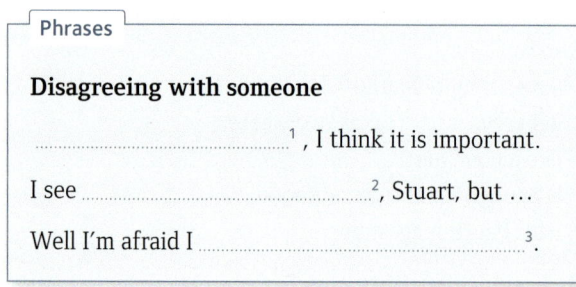
I don't agree (not I'm not agree)

8 Look at the dialogue again and complete the phrases below.

Phrases

Disagreeing with someone

....¹, I think it is important.

I see ....², Stuart, but …

Well I'm afraid I ....³.

9 Complete the dialogue with the words below. Who wants to change the deadline?

> actually · agree · don't agree · point

Oskar   Did we find a new date for the meeting?

Ralf   Yes, it is now on Friday at 9:00 a.m. I think we can finish everything by then.

Pauline   I think so too.

Oskar   Can I say something here? I think that's too early. We need more time to prepare.

Ralf   I'm afraid I ....¹, Oskar. We've had weeks to finish the project.

Oskar   Yes, but it would be good to have a few more days and do a better job.

Ralf   I see your ....², but we have a deadline. Pauline, what do you think?

Pauline   I ....³ with Oskar. A few more days would be good.

Ralf   ....⁴, I'm not sure we can change the deadline, but let me check.

10 🔊 14 A company is thinking about having a hot-desking policy. (Hot-desking is when people don't have their own desk, but instead share them and use one only when they need to.) Listen and tick the correct boxes below.

	Lisa	Dan	Jürgen	Raul	Beate
agree	☐	☐	☐	☐	☐
disagree	☐	☐	☐	☐	☐

> We should have a hot-desking policy.

Listen again and underline the word or phrase you hear.

1. I *completely/totally* agree. *In my opinion, / I think* it could make us more creative. More movement and ideas.
2. *Sorry, / I'm afraid* I don't agree. Hot-desking would make work more stressful.
3. *I see Jürgen's point / Jürgen has a point*, but it's important that we have space.
4. *How about / What about* five or six people at a desk?
   Actually,/Personally, I think it's a great idea.

Vocabulary

movement Bewegung
space Platz
to share teilen
stressful stressig

👥 What's your opinion? Would you like to work in an office with a hot-desking policy? Discuss with a partner.

11 👥 Have a meeting with your colleagues to discuss the problems below (or think of your own). Take turns making suggestions and agreeing or disagreeing.

1. You all work in the same office and it is too small.
2. Your team won't be able to meet an important deadline.

Why don't we			?
We should/could	have/make/…	…	.
Let's			
What about / How about	having/making/…		?

Key phrases

Here are some key phrases from the unit. Tick the ones that are useful for you.

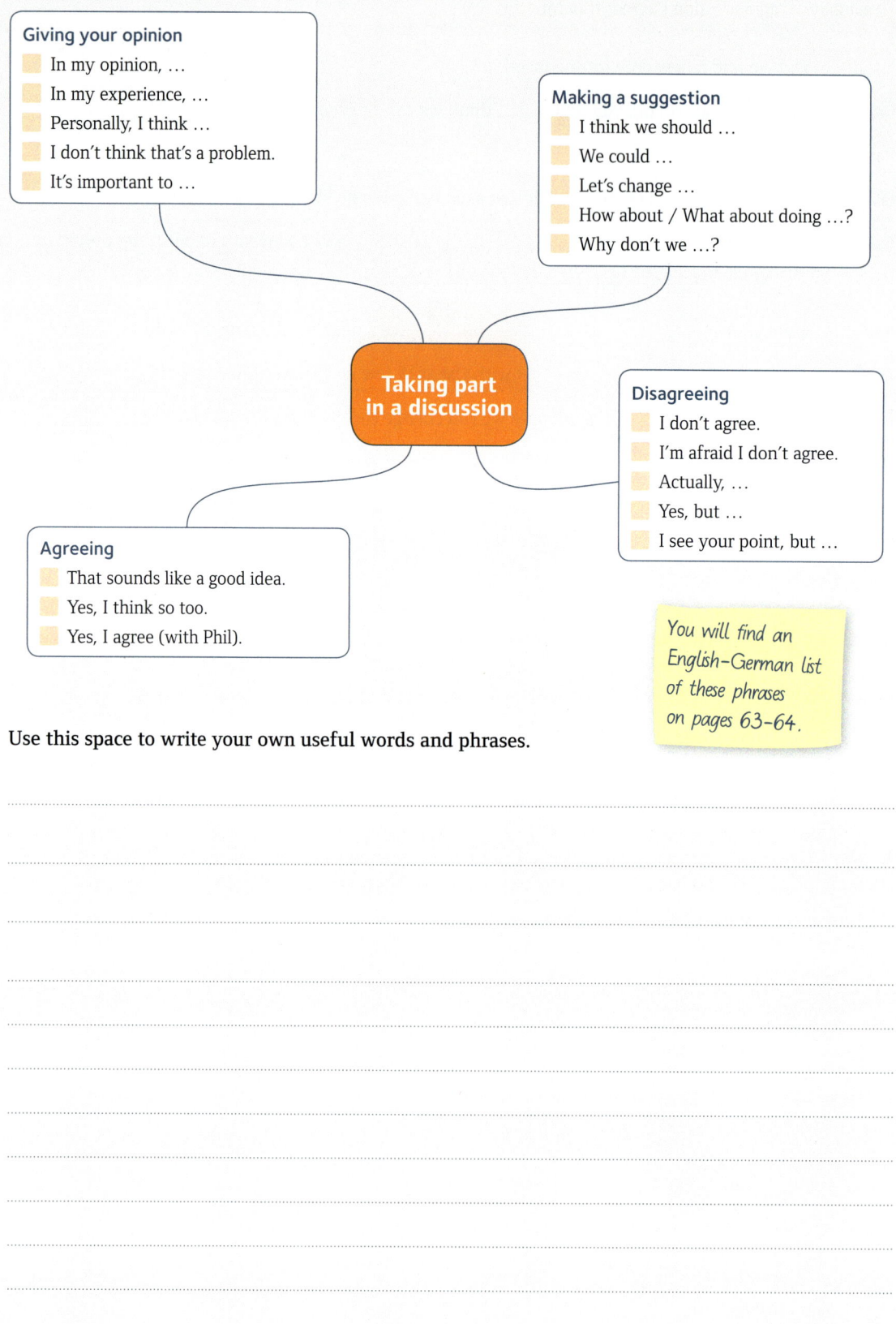

Giving your opinion
- In my opinion, …
- In my experience, …
- Personally, I think …
- I don't think that's a problem.
- It's important to …

Making a suggestion
- I think we should …
- We could …
- Let's change …
- How about / What about doing …?
- Why don't we …?

Taking part in a discussion

Disagreeing
- I don't agree.
- I'm afraid I don't agree.
- Actually, …
- Yes, but …
- I see your point, but …

Agreeing
- That sounds like a good idea.
- Yes, I think so too.
- Yes, I agree (with Phil).

You will find an English–German list of these phrases on pages 63–64.

Use this space to write your own useful words and phrases.

Over to you

12 Think of a typical meeting you go to. With a partner, think of the topics you might discuss there. Then, on your own, write down your opinion.

Discussion topics:

1 .... 2 ....

My opinion is:

....
....

Now work together again and practice the dialogue. When you finish, change roles and do the activity again.

A Give an opinion.

B Agree/Disagree with A's opinion and make a suggestion.

A Agree/Disagree with B's suggestion and suggest something new.

B Agree/Disagree.

Last but not least

13 Read the interview below.

The way people give their opinion or agree and disagree is different from country to country. Here's what Juan has to say. He's from Spain, but he works for a tech company in Berlin.

When you compare Spain to Germany, what differences do you see about the way people give an opinion?
Well, to start with, Germans say "no" more or they tell you directly when you are wrong. In Spain, people are not so direct when they disagree with you.

Do you think being direct is good or bad?
Being direct can sometimes be more productive. Everybody knows what you think. And being honest is really important too.

What advice would you give Germans working with people in Spain?
There are a few things I would say. If you're talking to Spanish people that you don't know well, disagreeing directly is not a good thing. You need to get to know them first, so it's better to find things you can agree on. Then, when you disagree, you should suggest an alternative solution and not just say "no, that's wrong".

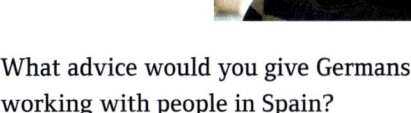

Vocabulary

to get to know sb. jdn. kennenlernen
honest ehrlich
relationship Beziehung
to try versuchen

Which point from the article is most important for Juan? Discuss the answers with your partner. Do you agree or disagree?

1 ☐ Being honest
2 ☐ Building relationships
3 ☐ Giving your opinion
4 ☐ Telling someone they are wrong
5 ☐ Trying to agree with each other

Learning objectives
- Describing a problem
  Ein Problem beschreiben
- Offering a solution
  Eine Lösung anbieten
- Delaying making a decision
  Eine Entscheidung hinauszögern

5 Problems and solutions

1 Have a look at the problems below and tick the ones you sometimes have to deal with.

- Missing a deadline
- Shipment delays
- Going over budget
- Personnel problems
- Communication problems

Vocabulary

to deal with sth. mit etw. umgehen
to go over budget ein Budget überschreiten
shipment Lieferung, Versand
to solve lösen

! personnel = Personal
personal = persönlich

Which type of problem is the most difficult to solve? Discuss with a partner.

2 🔊 15 Read and listen to the dialogue.
Which problem(s) do Axel and Lara discuss?

- Missing a deadline
- Going over budget
- Communication problems

Did you know?

Some people prefer not to use the word "problem". They often use words like "challenge", "issue", or "situation" as an alternative.

Axel	I wanted to update you on the project. I'm afraid we don't have enough parts left in the warehouse, which means we are going to have problems with the schedule.
Lara	So you're saying it's a supply issue, not a problem with the design?
Axel	Exactly. Everything is fine with the design. We just need extra time to get more parts.
Lara	OK, so what can we do?
Axel	Would it be possible to move the deadline?
Lara	Ah, that would be difficult. We need the first samples in two weeks. What about just getting 50 samples ready? Would that be possible by the deadline?
Axel	I'll have to check a few things, but I don't think that will be a problem.
Lara	And then we move the deadline for the rest to two weeks later. What do you think? Would that work?
Axel	Perfect. Thank you, and I'm very sorry for the delay.

Vocabulary

sample Probestück, Muster
supply Lieferung
warehouse Lager

3 🔊 16 Now read and listen to another dialogue. Put the topics in the order they are discussed.

- ☐ Selling online
- ☐ Summer special offer
- ☐ Sales of bestseller

Vocabulary

discount Rabatt
to reach erreichen
retailer (Einzel-)Händler/in
special offer Sonderangebot
unfortunately leider

Charlotte	We have a problem. Sales of our best-selling product are going down. Unfortunately, there's a new product on the market, and it's a lot cheaper. Shops think our quality is good, but our price is too high. What can we do?
Paula	Well, we have to think about how to reach customers.
Charlotte	Well, yes, but also about the price. What do you think, Werner?
Werner	We could sell it online …
Charlotte	Do you mean in our own shop or through other retailers?
Werner	Both, I think.
Paula	It's a good idea, but using other shops might be difficult. They often want big discounts.
Werner	True, but it might work. I'll see what information I can find about online retailers.
Charlotte	OK. Any other ideas?
Paula	Maybe we could have a special offer for the summer?
Charlotte	Excellent. I'll look into that.

4 Look at the dialogues in exercises 2 and 3 again and complete the phrases below.

Phrases

Describing a problem

I'm afraid ....¹ parts left in the warehouse …

We ....². Sales of our best-selling product are going down.

........................³, there's a new product on the market …

Looking for a solution

OK, so ....⁴ we do?

What ....⁵, Werner?

Any ....⁶?

Offering a solution

Would it ....⁷ to move the deadline?

What do you think? Would ....⁸?

We ....⁹ sell it online …

I'll ....¹⁰ I can find about online retailers.

5 Match the two parts of these sentences.

1 I'll see what
2 I'm afraid we
3 Would it be possible
4 What can we do to
5 Sorry, but it looks
6 Unfortunately,

a solve the problem?
b I can find out.
c to change the schedule?
d the shipment has been delayed.
e can't finish the project by May.
f like we are over budget.

6 Complete the dialogues with the phrases below.

> I'll look into · I'm afraid · we have a problem · What can we do?

1 A _____¹ there's a problem with the budget. We're still waiting for some of our customers to pay their invoices, which means we can't pay some of our own bills.
  B Oh. That's not good. _____²
  A We could send them an email and ask them about the delay.
  B Good idea. Thanks, Ralph.

2 A I'm afraid _____³. The project is delayed, and your team is not answering our calls.
  B So you're saying there is a communication problem. I'm really sorry about that. _____⁴ it today and see what the problem is.
  A Could you let me know as soon as you find anything out?
  B Of course.

Did you know?

When talking about difficulties, it's important to make sure you understand the other person correctly.

Do you mean we sent the customer the wrong product?

So you're saying that they want to cancel their order?

7 Two colleagues are discussing a problem. Work with a partner to put their sentences into the correct order (1–6). Then practice reading the dialogue out loud.

a So what can we do?

b Yes, I'm afraid that's correct. It was a stupid mistake and they're not going to be happy about it.

c We should call them right away. Do you think it would be possible to offer them a special deal on their next order?

d So you're saying they need to return them?

e Good idea. I'll have to check, but I think we can do that.

f We have a problem. Unfortunately, we sent Aldexco too many parts. [6]

English for Meetings

8 🔊 17 Read the four short dialogues below and complete the gaps with words from the box. Then listen and check.

Vocabulary
to get back to jdm. antworten
to hear back from sb. eine Antwort von jdm. bekommen
slide Präsentationsfolie

personnel · presentation · report · stand

1 A Have you finished preparing the slides for our ....¹ on Friday?
   B I'm sorry, I haven't finished them yet. Can I get back to you on Wednesday?

2 A Can we talk about the ....² that we need to write?
   B I'm afraid I don't have time today. Could we look at it tomorrow? I should have time then.

3 A What about having a larger ....³ at the trade fair this year?
   B It's difficult to say right now. Can we wait until we hear back from the organizers about prices?

4 A I'm afraid we don't have enough time now to talk about ....⁴ problems.
   B That's OK. Let's talk about them next week. We can invite someone from HR too.

9 Look at the dialogues in exercise 8 again and complete the phrases below.

Phrases

Delay making a decision

Can I ....¹ on Wednesday?

Could we ....² tomorrow?

Can we ....³ from the organizers about prices?

I'm afraid we don't have enough time … – That's OK. ....⁴ next week.

10 You are in a meeting and want to delay dealing with the tasks below. Use the table and your own ideas to make sentences, then compare them with a partner.

1 You don't have time to speak about the new prices.

2 You need to present the new product but have no time to finish the presentation today.

3 Your boss needs an update from the team in the U.S., but they haven't contacted you yet.

4 Your colleague asks for the sales figures. You haven't received the figures yet.

Let's	look at	that	next week/Monday/…	.
Can we / Could we	discuss / talk about	it / them	on Tuesday/Friday … / tomorrow / later	?
Can I	get back to you on that			
Can I/we	wait until I/we hear back from		…	

Unit 5 . Problems and solutions   33

Key phrases

Here are some key phrases from the unit. Tick the ones that are useful for you.

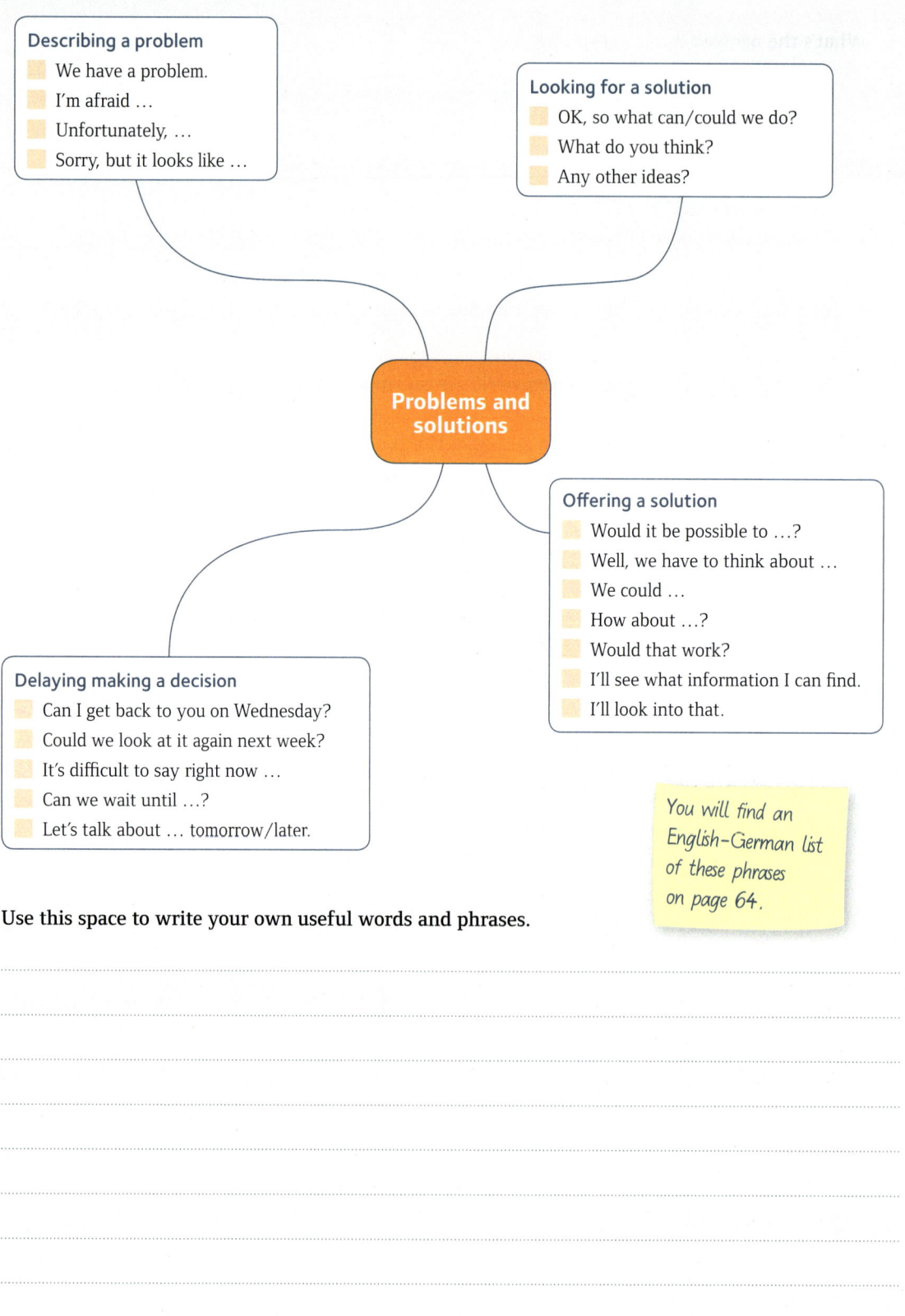

Describing a problem
- [ ] We have a problem.
- [ ] I'm afraid …
- [ ] Unfortunately, …
- [ ] Sorry, but it looks like …

Looking for a solution
- [ ] OK, so what can/could we do?
- [ ] What do you think?
- [ ] Any other ideas?

Problems and solutions

Offering a solution
- [ ] Would it be possible to …?
- [ ] Well, we have to think about …
- [ ] We could …
- [ ] How about …?
- [ ] Would that work?
- [ ] I'll see what information I can find.
- [ ] I'll look into that.

Delaying making a decision
- [ ] Can I get back to you on Wednesday?
- [ ] Could we look at it again next week?
- [ ] It's difficult to say right now …
- [ ] Can we wait until …?
- [ ] Let's talk about … tomorrow/later.

You will find an English–German list of these phrases on page 64.

Use this space to write your own useful words and phrases.

....
....
....
....
....
....

Over to you

11 With a partner, think of two problems you often have at work. Complete this table.

What's the problem?		
A solution could be …		

Practice the dialogue below using some of the key phrases from page 34. When you finish, change roles and do the activity again.

A Tell B about a problem and ask for a solution.

B Suggest a solution.

A Thank B but say you're not sure about the solution. Delay making a decision.

Last but not least

12 Read the text below. Do you think you are a solution-oriented person?

Vocabulary
self-starter jd. mit Eigeninitiative
to spend time on sth. sich mit etw. beschäftigen

Problems and solution-oriented people

Here are some tips for being more solution-oriented at work.

1 Focus on the solution (not the problem).
Ask yourself:
How can I solve this problem?
(not: Why do I have to do this?)

What is the first step we need to take to solve this problem? *(not: Why should I spend time on this?)*

What should we do to solve the problem?
(not: Who is responsible for the problem?)

2 Be a self-starter.
When you speak to your manager, explain the problem AND give your solution at the same time. Don't just describe the problem and ask "What do you think we should do?"

3 Talk less. Do more.
In meetings, if you answer the question "Is there a decision?" or "Is this task complete?" with "yes", then there is no need for any more discussion.

Do you find the advice in the text helpful? How do *you* solve problems? Do you have any other tips for dealing with problems? Discuss with a partner.

Learning objectives

- Starting a conference call
  Eine Telekonferenz starten
- Dealing with problems
  Mit Problemen umgehen
- Clarifying information
  Informationen klären

6 Conference calls

1 Read the advice for conference calls below. Which tips are for the person leading the call (L), which are for the participants (P), and which are for both (B)? Compare your answers with a partner. Can you think of any other tips?

☐ Make sure there are no technical problems.
☐ Use simple language.
☐ Call from a quiet place.
☐ Be on time.
☐ Say your name each time you speak.
☐ Send out an agenda before the meeting.

2 ◁ 18 Read and listen to the start of a conference call. Does everybody follow the advice above and in the box?

Enter your password ID, followed by the pound key. Thank you.
Password ID accepted. Please hold until the meeting organizer arrives.

Florian	Hello everyone, Florian here. Can everyone hear me OK?
John	Hello Florian, this is John. Yes, you're fine.
Nadja	Hi Florian, Nadja here. Yes, I can hear you.
Florian	Nadja, how is the weather there?
Nadja	Gray and wet. How about where you are?
Florian	It's sunny at the moment. Has Julien logged in yet?
John	John here. Not yet, but he should be here in a second.

Julien is entering the call.

Julien	Hi everyone, Julien here. Is the line OK?
Nadja	No, sorry, I can't hear you. Can you say that again?
Julien	This is Julien. Wait, I'll turn up my volume. How is that now?
Nadja	That's much better. Hello, Julien. Nadja, here.
Julien	Am I the last? Who else is here?
John	John. Hi.
Florian	And this is Florian. Hello. So, shall we get started then? Do you all have the agenda?
All	Yes.
Florian	OK, so today we want to talk about …

Did you know?

Conference calls can be difficult because you can't see the other people. Small talk at the beginning of the call can help you get familiar with people's voices and accents, and saying your name each time you speak makes sure everyone knows who's talking.

Vocabulary

to hold (the line) am Telefon bleiben
line Leitung, Verbindung
pound key Rautetaste
volume Lautstärke

What small-talk topic do the participants discuss? What other topics could they talk about at the start of the call? Discuss with a partner.

36   English for Meetings

3 🔊 19 Now read and listen to how the call continues. What is the problem?

a ☐ Nadja doesn't know Florian.
b ☐ Florian isn't speaking clearly.
c ☐ Nadja's connection is bad.

Vocabulary

connection Verbindung
to dial in sich einwählen
to hang up auflegen
worse schlimmer

Florian   OK, so today we want to talk about the Ramsfeld project. John, could you start?
Nadja   Wait a minute. This is Nadja. There's a problem with my line. Could you repeat that, please?
Florian   Nadja? Are you still there? I asked John to start.
Nadja   No, sorry, that's worse. I'll hang up and dial in again. One moment.
Nadja is entering the call.
Nadja   Nadja here. Does that sound better?
Florian   Florian. Yes, that's a lot clearer. So, let's begin. John, could you update us on the project? …

4 Look at exercises 2 and 3 again and complete the phrases below.

Phrases

Entering a call and getting started

Can ……………………¹ me OK?

Hello Florian, ……………………² John.

Hi Florian, Nadja here.

Has Julien ……………………³ yet?

Julien here. Is ……………………⁴ OK?

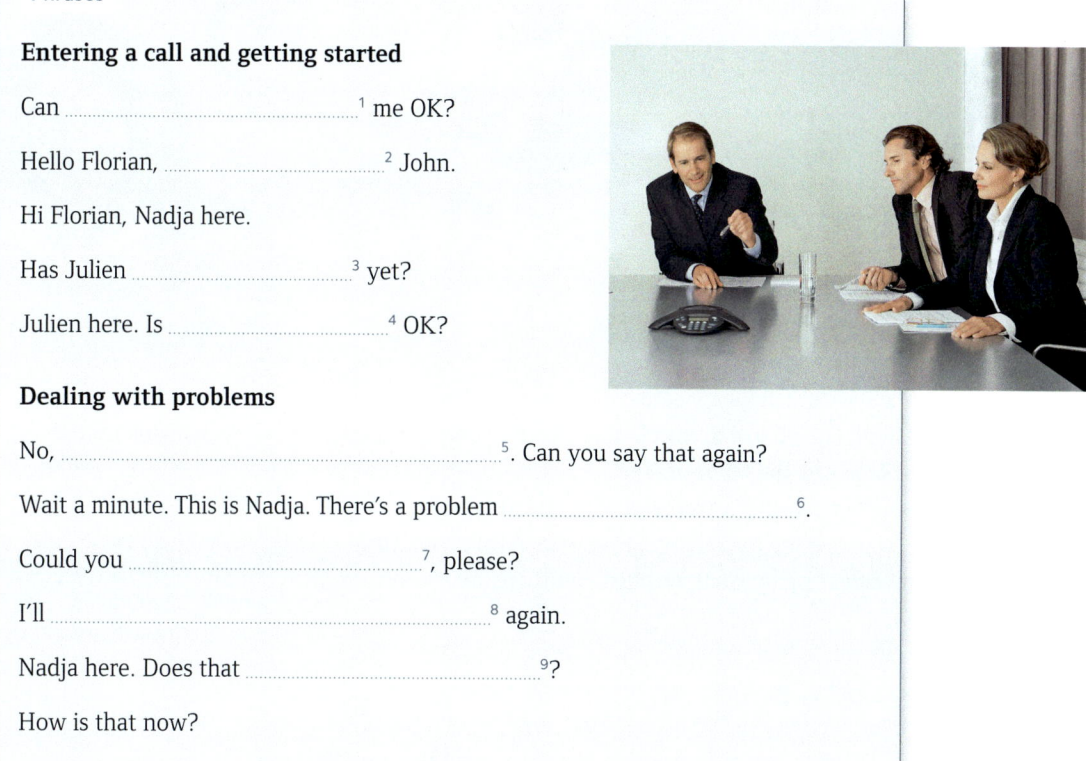

Dealing with problems

No, ……………………⁵. Can you say that again?

Wait a minute. This is Nadja. There's a problem ……………………⁶.

Could you ……………………⁷, please?

I'll ……………………⁸ again.

Nadja here. Does that ……………………⁹?

How is that now?

5 Match the sentences with a similar meaning.

1 Could you repeat that?
2 I'll hang up and dial in again.
3 No, sorry, I can't hear you.
4 There's a problem with my line.
5 Is everyone logged in?

a Are we all ready to begin?
b The connection isn't very good today.
c Could you say that again?
d One moment, let me try and call again.
e Sorry, I lost you. I didn't hear what you said.

Unit 6 . Conference calls   37

6 Fill in the missing words.

> about · for · in · in · up · up

1 Has everyone logged ...., or are we waiting .... anyone?

2 Paul, I can't hear you very well. Could you turn .... the volume?

3 Today, we wanted to talk .... reducing costs.

4 Sorry, now the connection's worse. I'm going to hang .... and dial .... again.

7 🔊 20 Read and listen to an extract from another conference call and say who …

1 is leading the meeting?
2 forgets to say his or her name?
3 has a problem understanding a difficult word?
4 will send everyone an email after the meeting?

Peter	I agree. It looks good.
Anika	Sorry, who's speaking?
Peter	Ah, sorry. Peter here.
Anika	Ah, Peter. Please say your name before speaking so we know who it is.
Peter	Sorry. So, as I said, things look good, and we should meet all our next milestones.
Anika	Thanks, Peter. That's great. Ralf, did you want to add anything to that?
Ralf	Yes, we're having a project meeting next week and we'll send you another update then.
Anika	Thanks, Ralf. OK, I'd like to turn to the next point on the agenda, which is changing the supplier. Tara, can you tell us more?
Tara	Well, we spoke about the problems with our supplier last week. So I'm looking for an alternative, which isn't easy. Only two firms offer exactly what we need, but there are downsides to both.
Ralf	Excuse me, this is Ralf. What do you mean by "downsides"?
Tara	Downsides? Uhm, problems, negative things. For example, one supplier has very high delivery costs, and the other is in Morocco, so too far away. It looks like we need to rethink our decision.
Anika	Anika here. Sorry, I didn't get the last part. Do you mean we need to rethink the decision to change suppliers? In other words, you think we should stay with our current supplier.
Tara	Yes, unfortunately, I do.
Peter	Peter here. Can I say something here? I think it would be good for us all to look at the alternatives before we make a decision. Tara, could you send us an email with the details of the other suppliers?
Ralf	Ralf here. I agree with Peter. It would be good to see the details, Tara.
Tara	No problem. I'll send them this afternoon.
Anika	OK, so Tara will send us the details about the firms. But, just to be clear, only the details for the two suppliers we talked about. OK, so let's look at our last point for today …

Vocabulary

downside Nachteil
milestone Meilenstein
to rethink überdenken
to turn to sth. sich etw. zuwenden

8 Look at the dialogue again and complete the phrases below.

> **Phrases**
>
> **Clarifying information**
>
> Sorry, ...¹ speaking?
>
> Ralf, did you want to ....² to that?
>
> Excuse me, this is Ralf. ....³ "downsides"?
>
> Sorry, I ....⁴ the last part.
>
> ....⁵, you think we should stay with our current supplier.
>
> But, ...⁶, only the details for the two suppliers …

! current = aktuell
actual = eigentlich

9 Look at these extracts from three conference calls and complete them with the phrases below.

> do you mean • excuse me • I didn't get • in other words • just to be clear • who's speaking

1 A So, about the Fedun project …
   B Sorry, ...¹?
   A It's Richard. Unfortunately, we are going to miss one of our milestones in the Fedun project, but it shouldn't be a problem.
   C ....², this is Rachel. ....³, which milestone are you talking about?

2 A Could you tell us the status of your report, Benjamin?
   B ....⁴ the report on the project in Cologne?
   A Yes, that's right.

3 A Sorry, ...⁵ the last part. What did you say?
   B I said that the Trespas team will arrive a bit later.
   A ....⁶, we'll meet them after lunch?
   B Yes, exactly. At 2:00 p.m.

meinen = mean
Meinen Sie dieses Projekt?
= Do you mean this project?
meinen = think
Ich meine, wir haben ein Problem.
= I think we have a problem.

10 What would you say in these situations? Match the phrases (a–f) to the situations (1–6).

1 ☐ Somebody uses a word you don't know.
2 ☐ You don't know who just said something.
3 ☐ You can't hear a participant who just dialed in.
4 ☐ You missed the end of what someone said.
5 ☐ You want to see if anyone has something else to say.
6 ☐ You want to make sure you understand someone's suggestion.

a Do you want to add anything?
b So, in other words, you think we need to change the schedule?
c I didn't get the last part. What did you say?
d Sorry, who's speaking?
e Could you turn up the volume?
f Excuse me, but what does that mean?

🗣 Think of other phrases you can say in each situation. Compare your answers with a partner.

Unit 6 . Conference calls 39

Key phrases

Here are some key phrases from the unit. Tick the ones that are useful for you.

Entering a call and getting started
- Can everyone hear me OK?
- Hello Florian, this is John.
- Hi Florian, Nadja here.
- Is everyone logged in?
- Are we all ready to begin?
- Is the line OK?
- Shall we get started then?

Dealing with problems
- Sorry, I can't hear you. Can you say that again?
- Could you repeat that, please?
- Could you turn up the volume, please?
- Wait a minute. There's a problem with my line.
- I'll hang up and dial in again.
- Does that sound better?
- That's a lot clearer.

Conference calls

Clarifying information
- Sorry, who's speaking?
- Did you want to add anything to that?
- Excuse me. What do you mean by …?
- Sorry, I didn't get that / the last part.
- Do you mean we should …?
- In other words, …
- Just to be clear, …

You will find an English–German list of these phrases on page 65.

Use this space to write your own useful words and phrases.

Over to you

11 In groups of three, take part in a conference call. Answer the questions below to prepare.

Who is taking part in the call? ....

What is on the agenda? ....

What things might need clarifying? ....

Note down some phrases you would like to use.

Say that you are on the line: ....

Make some small talk: ....

Ask a question to clarify something: ....

Now practice the call, using the prompts below. When you finish, discuss how the call went. Were there any things that needed clarifying?

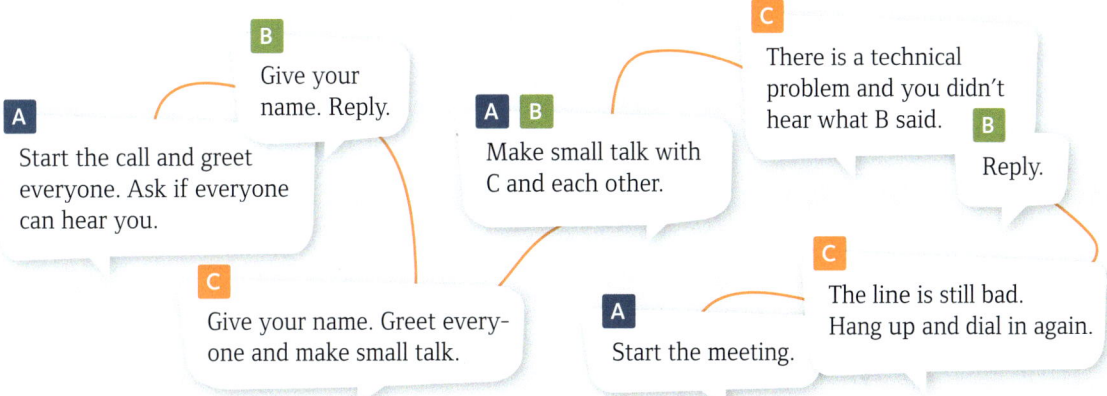

Last but not least

12 Read the tips on taking part in a conference call. What advice do you agree with?

Vocabulary

body language Körpersprache
now and then ab und zu
shy schüchtern
successful gelungen

Successful conference calls

- You don't have to talk all the time, but try to ask a question or give your opinion now and then. If you are too quiet, the other participants could think that you are unhappy or doing something else during the call (like checking emails!).
- If other people are talking too much and you would like to say something, you can say "Excuse me" or "Can I say something here?" You could also use someone's name in the question you ask, e.g. "Ralph, what do you think of the timeline?" Using names is

important in conference calls because you can't use body language.
- If you are shy, especially when there are a lot of people on the call, you could call the moderator (or "meeting organizer") before the conference call begins. You can then explain what you want to say later during the call.
- Find a quiet room for your call. The last thing you want is to be in the back of a taxi, on the way to the airport or in a loud office.

How do you prepare for conference calls? Add your own tips and discuss them with a partner.

Unit 6 . Conference calls 41

7 Arranging a meeting

Learning objectives
- Arranging a meeting by phone and email
  Eine Besprechung per Telefon und E-Mail organisieren
- Rearranging a meeting
  Eine Besprechung verschieben

1 How do you invite participants to a meeting? Tick the options. Are there any you can add? Compare your answers with a partner.

- over the phone
- by text message
- using a calendar invitation
- by email

- other ....

Vocabulary

invitation Einladung
to invite sb. jdn. einladen

2 ◁ 21 Jana calls a colleague to arrange a meeting. Read and listen, then say when she and Bruce are meeting and why.

Bruce	Good morning, Bruce speaking.
Jana	Hello, Bruce. It's Jana here.
Bruce	Jana, hi. What can I do for you?
Jana	Well, the team from Adriatico are coming next week, and it would be good to talk about our strategy before the meeting. So, could we meet on Thursday?
Bruce	Good idea, but I'm afraid I can't make Thursday. How about Friday afternoon at 2:00?
Jana	That's fine, but I might be a few minutes late. I have a meeting at 1:30.
Bruce	Why don't we say 2:15 then?
Jana	Yes, that sounds good. Thanks, Bruce. See you on Friday.
Bruce	See you then. Bye.

It's Jana (here). (not ~~Here is Jana.~~)

Did you know?

The 24-hour clock is not used very often in the English-speaking world. It is better to say "in the morning/afternoon" or "a.m./p.m.".
6:00 = six o'clock in the morning / six a.m.
18:00 = six o'clock in the afternoon / six p.m.
12:00 = noon (AE) / midday (BE)
24:00 = midnight

42 English for Meetings

3 Silvia writes an email to invite a business partner to a meeting. Read the email, then answer true or false.

		True	False
1	The invitation is for a second meeting.	☐	☐
2	Silvia is from the Human Resources department.	☐	☐
3	The meeting is planned for Friday.	☐	☐
4	The meeting will take place at a hotel in Bremen.	☐	☐

Vocabulary

follow-up Folge-, nachfolgend
to get in touch sich melden
impressed beeindruckt
to set up arrangieren

To: kelly.richards@easysolutions.com
From: schmidt_silvia@TRS.de
Subject: **Invitation to a follow-up meeting**

Dear Kelly,

Thank you for meeting with me on Monday.

I was very impressed by your company's IT solutions. I talked about them to our HR department, and they would like to arrange a meeting to test some of your products.

We would like to set up a meeting on Tuesday, October 25 at 10:00 in our Bremen office. Could you let me know by Friday if that would work for you?

Please get in touch if you have any questions.

I look forward to seeing you again soon.

Best wishes,
Silvia

Did you know?

Emails in English always start with a capital letter.
Dear Kelly,
Thank you …

I look forward to
seeing you again.
(not ~~to see you again~~)

4 Look at the phone call and the email again and complete the phrases below.

Phrases

Arranging a meeting by phone

So, ...¹ meet on Thursday?

I'm afraid I ....² Thursday. ....³ Friday afternoon at 2:00?

That's fine, but I ....⁴ a few minutes late.

Why ....⁵ 2:15 then?

Arranging a meeting by email

We ....⁶ a meeting on Tuesday, October 25 …

Could you ....⁷ Friday if that would work for you?

Please ....⁸ if you have any questions.

I look forward ....⁹ again soon.

5 Match the sentence halves.

1. Would it be possible to
2. Could you let us know
3. I look forward to
4. Could we set up a
5. Would 9:00 or 9:30
6. Why don't we say

work better for you?
3:00 p.m. then?
meet on Wednesday afternoon instead?
by Friday at the latest?
meeting next Tuesday in my office?
seeing you on Friday.

Now match the sentences to these replies.

a ☐ Yes, me too. See you then!
b ☐ Yes, I'll talk to my colleagues and email you on Thursday.
c ☐ Sorry, I can't make Tuesday. How about Thursday instead?
d ☐ Sounds good. Wednesday at 2:00 p.m. would work for me.
e ☐ Three o'clock in your office? Sounds great.
f ☐ Half past nine would be great.

> 9:30
> = "half past nine"
> or "half nine" (BE)

6 Complete the email with the phrases below.

best wishes · get in touch · let me know · look forward · set up a meeting · thanks for

Dear Petra,

.................¹ your email.

I'd like to ....² for next week to talk about the budget for the project with Hurricane. Would Wednesday at 11:00 be OK for you? Could you ....³ by tomorrow if you can make it?

Please ....⁴ if you have any questions.

I ....⁵ to seeing you soon.

.................⁶,
Mike

7 Mike writes another email to a colleague he knows well. Put the parts of the email into the correct order (1–4).

Hi Rasmus,
  ☐ a Let me know!
  ☐ b Can we meet on Thursday at 10:30 to work on the report?
  ☐ c I hope you had a good weekend.
  ☐ d If you can't make the morning, the afternoon would also be good for me.
Thanks,
Mike

Did you know?
Emails to people outside the company are usually – but not always – more formal than emails to colleagues. If you're not sure how formal your email should be, use the same style as the person who wrote to you.

👥 Now compare the two emails. What is similar and what is different? Discuss with a partner.

8 🔊22 Sometimes plans change. Read and listen to the short dialogues below. Why do the people need to rearrange their meetings? When are they planning to meet now?

1 A Oh, Sarah, do have a minute? I'm really sorry. I have to cancel our meeting this afternoon. I have an urgent appointment with a client.
  B That's too bad. Can we meet at another time then?
  A Yes, of course. How about Monday at 3:00 p.m.?
  B Sorry, but Monday doesn't work for me. I'll be away. How about Tuesday morning?
  A Tuesday morning? Let me see. Yes, I should be free then. Can you make nine o'clock?
  B Sounds good, Theo. So that's Tuesday at 9:00 a.m. Great. I'll update it in the computer.

2 A I'm sorry, but I can't take your call right now. Please leave a message.
  B Hi John, it's Marion. I got your message about cancelling the meeting this afternoon. I just want to confirm that I can make Monday at two o'clock. I'm sorry that you are not feeling well and hope you feel better soon! Bye.

> I have an *appointment*.
> (not ~~I have a date.~~)

Vocabulary

appointment Termin
to cancel absagen
to confirm zusagen, bestätigen
urgent dringend

9 Look at the dialogues again and complete the phrases below.

Phrases

Rearranging a meeting

I _____¹ our meeting this afternoon.

That's too bad. _____² another time then?

Unfortunately, I can't make the meeting today.

Can you make it on another day?

Sorry, but Monday _____³ for me.

Tuesday morning? Let me see. Yes, I _____⁴ then.

Confirming the day and time

_____⁵ Tuesday at 9:00 a.m. Great.

I just _____⁶ that I can make Monday at 2:00.

I'll send you an email to confirm.

10 🔊23 Choose the correct words to complete the dialogue. Then listen and check.

A Claire, listen. I'm sorry, but I can't *arrange/make*¹ the meeting tomorrow. I have an urgent *appointment/date*² with a client. Can we *attend/meet*³ at another time?
B Don't worry, Mario. *How/Why*⁴ about Friday at 1:00 p.m.?
A Friday sounds good. I *might/should*⁵ be free then.
B Perfect. So, *it's/that's*⁶ Friday at one o'clock. See you *then/later*⁷. Bye.

Key phrases

Here are some key phrases from the unit. Tick the ones that are useful for you.

Arranging a meeting
- [ ] Could/Can we meet on Friday morning at 9:00?
- [ ] How about Monday at 3:00 p.m.?
- [ ] What about Tuesday morning?
- [ ] Why don't we say 2:15 then?

Arranging a meeting by email (formal/neutral)
- [ ] We would like to set up a meeting on Tuesday, October 25.
- [ ] Could you let me know by Friday if that would work for you / if you can make it?
- [ ] Would Wednesday at 11:00 be OK for you?
- [ ] Please get in touch if you have any questions.
- [ ] I look forward to seeing you (again soon).

Saying you can or can't attend
- [ ] Thursday morning after 10:00 a.m. would work (for me).
- [ ] Tuesday sounds good.
- [ ] I'm afraid I can't make Friday.
- [ ] Sorry, I can't make 2:00 p.m.
- [ ] Sorry, but Monday doesn't work for me.

Arranging a meeting by email (informal)
- [ ] Can we meet on Thursday at 10:30 to work on …?
- [ ] Let me know (if you can make it).

Arranging meeting

Rearranging a meeting
- [ ] I'm really sorry. I have to cancel our meeting this afternoon.
- [ ] I have an urgent appointment.
- [ ] Unfortunately, I can't come to the meeting today / tomorrow / next week.
- [ ] Can you make it on another day?
- [ ] Would it be possible to meet on/at … instead?
- [ ] Let me see. Yes, I should be free then.

Confirming a meeting
- [ ] So that's Tuesday at 9:00 a.m. Great.
- [ ] I'll send you an email to confirm.
- [ ] I just want to confirm that I can make Monday at 2:00.

You will find an English-German list of these phrases on page 66.

Use this space to write your own useful words and phrases.

....
....
....
....
....
....
....

Over to you

11 Work with a partner and practice arranging a meeting over the phone or face to face. When you finish, change roles and do the activity again.

A Invite B to a meeting. Say when, where and why you want to meet.

B You can't make the day. Suggest a different one.

A Agree to the day, but suggest a different time.

B Agree.

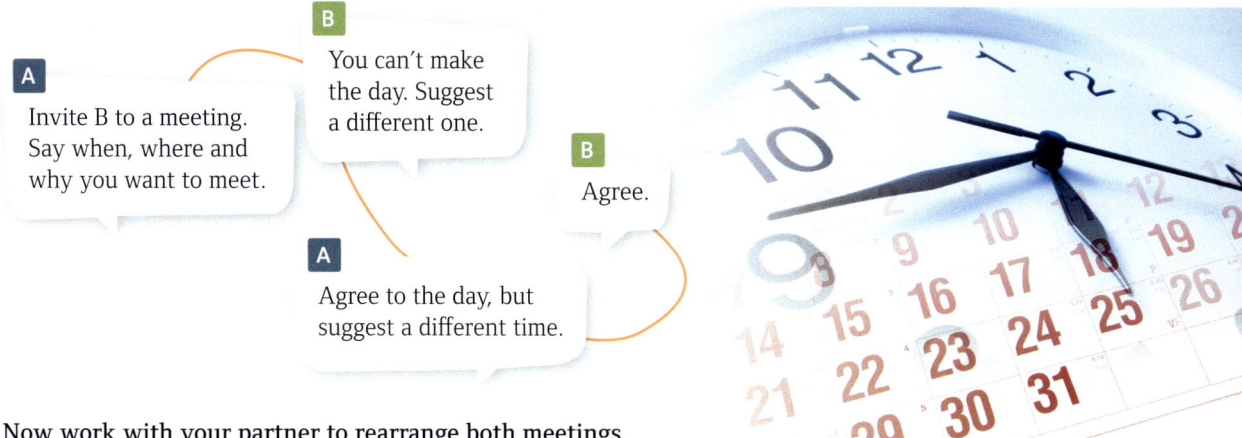

Now work with your partner to rearrange both meetings.

12 Think of the people you often meet with and write an email to invite one of them to a meeting. Exchange emails with a partner. Is your partner's email to a business partner or a colleague? How can you tell?

Last but not least

13 Have a look at this online forum. Have you experienced something similar?

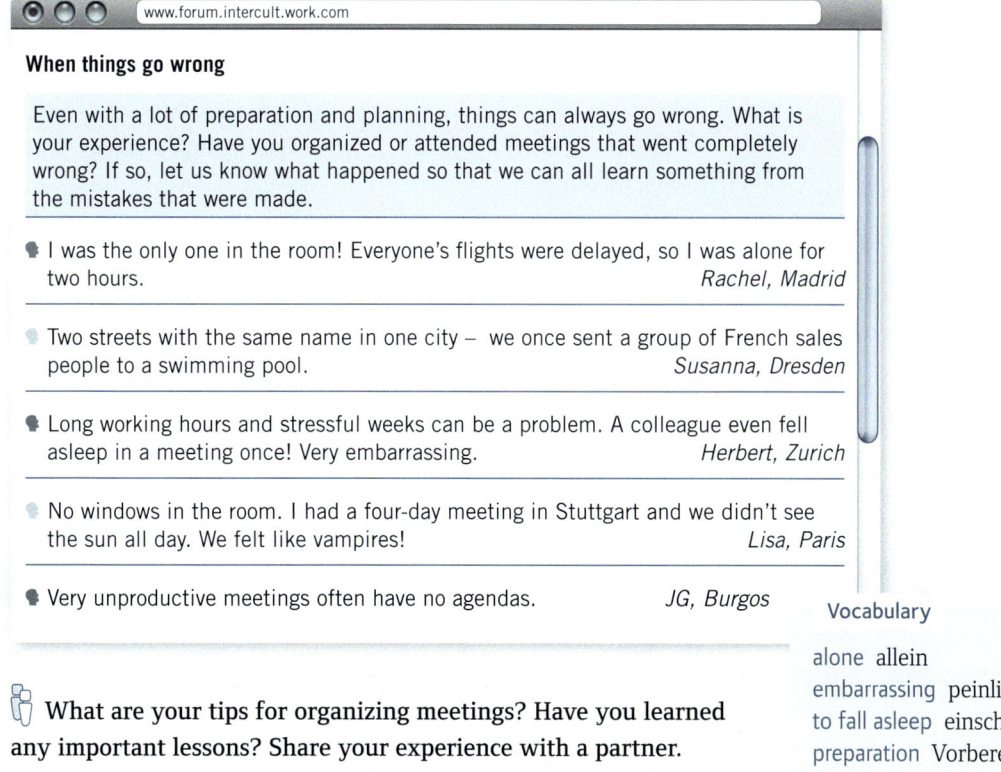

What are your tips for organizing meetings? Have you learned any important lessons? Share your experience with a partner.

Vocabulary

alone allein
embarrassing peinlich
to fall asleep einschlafen
preparation Vorbereitung

Learning objectives
- Opening and closing a meeting
  Eine Besprechung anfangen und beenden
- Asking for comments and delegating tasks
  Um Stellungnahmen bitten und Aufgaben delegieren

8 Leading a meeting

1 Meetings often follow a fixed structure. With a partner, look at some of the chairperson's tasks below and decide when he or she does them: at the beginning (B), in the middle (M), or at the end (E) of the meeting.

	B	M	E
1 Help with decision-making			
2 Summarize the main points			
3 Introduce the agenda			
4 Welcome everybody			
5 Thank participants for their work			
6 Ask somebody to take the minutes			
7 Get feedback from everyone			
8 Explain the reason for having the meeting			
9 Talk about action points and delegate tasks			
10 Check the time			

Vocabulary

to chair (a meeting) leiten
chairperson Vorsitzende/r
to summarize
   zusammenfassen

Did you know?

The term "action points" is used to talk about the tasks that one person or a group of people needs to do after a meeting.

What experience do you have of chairing a meeting?
Tell your partner.

2 ◁ 24 Andrew is chairing a team meeting. Read and listen. Which four tasks from the list above does he do?

Vocabulary

to move on to sth.
   zu etw. übergehen
progress report
   Zwischenbericht
proposal Vorschlag, Angebot

Andrew   Great. Let's get started. OK, so thank you very much for coming today. Can someone please take the minutes?
Mindy   I'm happy to do that.
Andrew   Thanks, Mindy.
Mindy   No problem.
Andrew   So, we're here today to talk about strategy for AISCO. The first item on the agenda is a progress report from Adam. Then we'll move on to the proposal.
Kirsten Sorry, I'm late everyone. I hope I didn't miss too much.
Andrew   No problem, Kirsten. We're just going through the agenda. Take a seat. So, after the proposal, Mindy will present some feedback from our consultants. And finally, we'll talk about the next milestones. OK, so we'll start with the progress report. Adam, do you want to tell us about that?
Adam   Yes, thanks. I'm going to look at our progress in the past six months. Things are looking good …

English for Meetings

Read or listen again and add the two missing items to the agenda.

Agenda Items			
1	Progress report (Adam)	3	Feedback from consultants (Mindy)
2	.... (Andrew)	4	.... (all)

3 Look at the dialogue again and complete the sentences below.

> **Phrases**
>
> **Introducing the agenda**
>
> So, ...¹ to talk about strategy for AISCO.
>
> The ....² is a progress report from Adam.
>
> Then ....³ the proposal.
>
> After the proposal, Mindy will present some feedback from our consultants.
>
> And ....⁴ the next milestones.

She will present (some) feedback.
(not a feedback)

Did you know?
It is common to use *will* to tell people the meeting topics.
First, we will ... Then we'll ... Finally, Sam will ...

First ...
Next ...
Then ...

4 Put the words into the correct order to make sentence beginnings.

1 here | We're | talk about ... | today | to ....

2 item | first | on | the agenda | is ... | The ....

3 we'll | move | to | on ... | Then ....

4 look at ... | we will | that | After ....

5 talk | about ... | Finally, | we'll ....

5 You are chairing a meeting. Use the sentence beginnings above to go through an agenda. (You can use the agenda below if you like.) Compare your opening with a partner.

Team meeting: selling our new product

Agenda Items
1 Market situation (Fiona)
2 Presentation: what other companies offer (Sam)
3 Information on our new online sales strategy (Sue)
4 New product name? (all)
5 Misc.

Unit 8 . Leading a meeting   49

6 🔊 25 **Listen to the last part of the meeting. What is the problem?**

a ☐ Nobody took the minutes.   c ☐ There's a meeting next week.
b ☐ They don't have enough time.

Andrew	So, we've looked at the milestones. Does everyone agree with them?
Mindy	Yes.
Adam	Me too.
Kirsten	I agree too, but could we talk about our tasks on this project, because …?
Andrew	Can I stop you there? Unfortunately, we don't have much time left.
Kirsten	OK, then can we add this to the agenda for next week?
Andrew	That's a good idea. What does everyone else think? Mindy? Adam?
Adam	I agree with Kirsten that we need to talk about the tasks.
Mindy	Me too.
Andrew	We'll add it to next week's agenda then. Adam, can you do that? Thanks. So, to summarize, today we talked about the strategy for the next six months and we decided on our proposal. And now, the action points. Kirsten will send me information about the contract for AISCO and Adam will follow up on their offer. Mindy, do you have all that?
Mindy	Yes, I do.
Andrew	So, you'll send us the minutes. And Adam, you're responsible for next week's agenda.
Adam	And the first item will be to discuss tasks.
Kirsten	Great, thanks.
Andrew	Please send Adam any other points by Wednesday noon. So, that's all we have time for. Thanks for coming. See you next week.

👥 **Which tasks from the list in exercise 1 does Andrew do in this part of the meeting? Discuss with a partner.**

Vocabulary

to follow up on sth.
   etw. nachverfolgen
offer   Angebot

7 **Look at the dialogue again and complete the sentences below.**

> **Phrases**
>
> **Asking for feedback**
>
> So, we've looked at the milestones. Does everyone _____¹ them?
>
> What does _____² think?
>
> **Checking the time**
>
> Can I stop you there? Unfortunately, we don't have _____³.
>
> So, that's all we _____⁴.
>
> **Summarizing a meeting and delegating tasks**
>
> So, _____⁵, today we talked about …
>
> Let me just summarize what we discussed today.
>
> Kirsten will send me information about …, and Adam will follow up on …
>
> And Adam, you're _____⁶ next week's agenda.

English for Meetings

8 🔊 26 **Complete these extracts from a meeting with the phrases below. Then listen and check.**

> agree with that · can finish there · for coming · have time for ·
> put it on · quickly summarize · the minutes from · think we should

1 A So, you _____¹ talk to the client about changing the deadline? Does everyone else _____ _____²?

B Yes, it's a good idea.

C I agree.

2 A Excuse me, but can we discuss the timeline now?

B Sorry, I'm afraid that's all we _____³ today. Let's _____⁴ next week's agenda.

3 A Let me just _____⁵. We decided on the launch date and we discussed the milestones for the new project. Is there anything else?

B No, that's everything.

4 A So, I think we _____⁶. Holger, could you send everyone _____ _____⁷ today?

B Sure, no problem. I can do it this afternoon.

A Great. So, thanks _____⁸, everyone. See you next time.

9 **You are chairing a meeting. Work with a partner to decide what you can say in the situations below. Look at the example first.**

> You want someone to take the minutes.

> Lina, could you take the minutes today please?

1 You want to make sure everybody likes a suggestion that a participant just made.
2 You want to know what two very quiet people think about the plan you are discussing.
3 There's no time left. You want somebody to finish his or her point so you can end the meeting.
4 You want to go over the main points you discussed in the meeting.
5 You want one of the participants to prepare the agenda for the next meeting.
6 You want to thank the participants and close the meeting.

Key phrases

Here are some key phrases from the unit. Tick the ones that are useful for you.

Introducing the agenda
- Let's start.
- So, we're here today to talk about …
- The first item on the agenda is …
- We'll start with …
- Then, we'll move on to …
- After that, we will look at …
- And finally, we'll talk about …

Asking for feedback
- Does everyone agree with the milestones / the decision?
- Mary, do you agree?
- What do you think, John?
- What does everyone else think?

Checking the time
- Can I stop you there?
- Unfortunately, we don't have much time left.
- Let's put that on next week's agenda.

Leading a meeting

Delegating tasks
- Can you send everyone the minutes from today?
- Kirsten will send me information about …, and Adam will follow up on …
- Adam, you're responsible for …

Summarizing and closing a meeting
- So, that's all we have time for today.
- I think we should stop / can finish there.
- Let me just (quickly) summarize what we discussed today.
- So, to summarize, today we talked about …
- Thanks for coming. See you next time/week.

You will find an English-German list of these phrases on page 67.

Use this space to write your own useful words and phrases.

....
....
....
....
....
....
....

Over to you

10 Think of a typical meeting you have to chair. Write down the topics you want to talk about with the meeting participants.

Item 1 ....

Item 2 ....

Item 3 ....

Now think about what you can say to do the following.

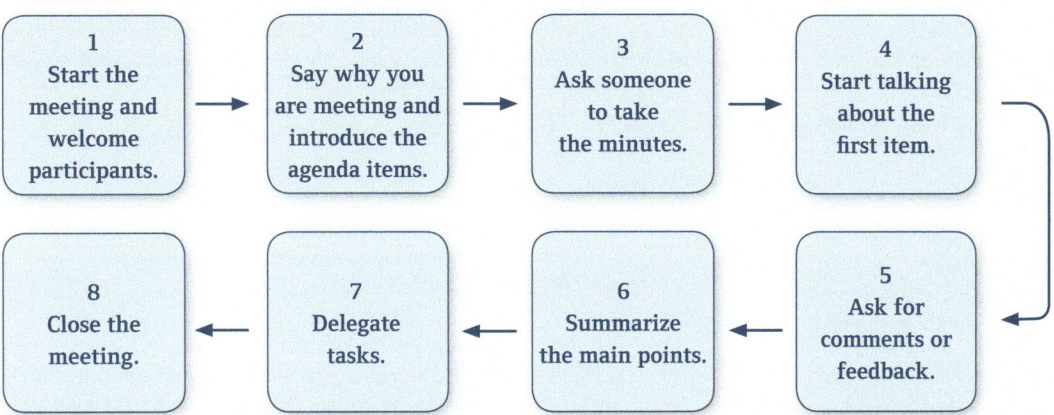

11 Work with a partner. Take turns being the chair and practice opening and closing a meeting.

Last but not least

12 Below are some tips for leading meetings. Read what people say and see if you agree.

> Keep to your agenda. Sometimes people want to add new items to the agenda. This can make your meetings a lot longer, so say no.

> Some people believe meetings are a chance to chat. Discussion is good, but it's important to stop people from speaking too much. Saying something like "Let's come back to …" usually helps. Stay polite and try to make positive suggestions.

> Everyone should get the chance to speak. If you want to include somebody, speak to them directly, for example saying something like "What do you think, Karsten?"

> Action points need to be clear, and the chairperson should check that people do their tasks after the meeting.

> Ask difficult questions like "How do you think this will work?" People need to think about their ideas. If you chair a meeting, you organize and you lead.

What tips would you add? What lessons have you learned from leading or attending meetings? Discuss with a partner.

Vocabulary

chance Gelegenheit
to keep to sth. sich an etw. halten

Transcripts

Unit 1   Exercise 6   04

Dialogue 1

A Hello, Sven. Nice to see you. How are you?
B Hi, David. I'm well, thanks. And you?
A Me too, especially now the weather is so good. And how was your trip?
B It was fine, thanks.

Dialogue 2

A Hello, I'm Renate. It's nice to finally meet you, Mr. Martinez.
B And you. Please call me Javier. This is my colleague, Maria Lopez.
C It's nice to meet you.
A Pleasure to meet you. Is this your first time in Germany?
C Yes, it is, but I've wanted to come for a while.

Dialogue 3

A Hi everyone. How are you all?
B/C/D Good. / Well, thanks.
A Great, then please take a seat and we'll get started.

Unit 2   Exercise 8   08

Laura Ah, here's Michael now.
Michael Yes, sorry I'm late. Thank you for waiting, and thank you all for coming. So, let's get started. Shall we go through the agenda first?
Attendees Yes. / OK.
Michael Excellent. Arne, can you take the minutes today?
Arne Of course.
Michael Thanks. So, the main items on the agenda are updates from both of our teams: from our team, on the budget and the problems we're having with our computer system, and from Dan-Design, …
Hilda Sorry, Michael. Could you also update us on the changes in your company?
Michael That's a good point. I can say a few words about that. Let me just add that to the agenda, before the budget, OK? … Are there any other points we should add?
Laura Yes, I have a point for miscellaneous. I think we need to discuss …

Unit 4   Exercise 10   14

Sarah So to help us with some of the space problems in the office at the moment, someone suggested we have a hot-desking policy. What does everyone think? Lisa?
Lisa I completely agree. I think it could make us more creative. More movement and ideas. Sounds great to me.
Sarah What about you, Dan?
Dan Sorry, I don't agree. Hot-desking would make work more stressful. I need to sit with my team. It would be difficult without them.
Sarah Jürgen?
Jürgen Personally, I think it sounds like a good idea. It's nice to look at something different every day.
Sarah Raul, what do you think?
Raul I see Jürgen's point, but it's important that we have space. The office is too small.
Beate So, we can use large desks. What about five or six people at a desk? Actually, I think it's a great idea. Let's do it!
Sarah Thanks, Beate. Thanks for your opinions, everyone. Let's think about it and talk again next week.

Unit 5   Exercise 8   17

1

A Have you finished preparing the slides for our presentation on Friday?
B I'm sorry, I haven't finished them yet. Can I get back to you on Wednesday?

2

A Can we talk about the report that we need to write?
B I'm afraid I don't have time today. Could we look at it tomorrow? I should have time then.

3

A What about having a larger stand at the trade fair this year?
B It's difficult to say right now. Can we wait until we hear back from the organizers about prices?

4

A I'm afraid we don't have enough time now to talk about personnel problems.
B That's OK. Let's talk about them next week. We can invite someone from HR too.

Unit 7 Exercise 10 ◁23

A Claire, listen. I'm sorry, but I can't make the meeting tomorrow. I have an urgent appointment with a client. Can we meet at another time?
B Don't worry, Mario. How about Friday at 1:00 p.m.?
A Friday sounds good. I should be free then.
B Perfect. So, that's Friday at one o'clock. See you then. Bye.

Unit 8 Exercise 8 ◁26

1

A So, you think we should talk to the client about changing the deadline? Does everyone else agree with that?
B Yes, it's a good idea.
C I agree.

2

A Excuse me, but can we discuss the timeline now?
B Sorry, I'm afraid that's all we have time for today. Let's put it on next week's agenda.

3

A Let me just quickly summarize. We decided on the launch date and we discussed the milestones for the new project. Is there anything else?
B No, that's everything.

4

A So, I think we can finish there. Holger, could you send everyone the minutes from today?
B Sure, no problem. I can do it this afternoon.
A Great. So, thanks for coming, everyone. See you next time.

Answer key

Unit 1

Exercise 1
a 1   b 2, 3

Exercise 2
the trip, the weather

Exercise 3
Rob and Anja, Anja and Lina

Exercise 4
1 You **must be** Ms. Kowalski.
2 It's **a pleasure** to meet you.
3 It's **nice to meet** you (too).
4 Nice to **see you again**.
5 Good thanks, **and with** you?
6 **I'm** Susanne Müller.
7 Please **call me** Magda.
8 This **is my colleague**, Lina Pohl.
9 So, **please take** a seat.
10 Would **you like** some coffee?

Exercise 5
1 d 2 e 3 a 4 b 5 f 6 c

Exercise 6
1 a 2 b 3 a 4 a 5 b 6 b

Exercise 7
1 It's nice to see you both again.
2 How are things?
3 This is Natascha Eder.
4 It's a pleasure to meet you.
5 So, let's get started.
6 Would anyone like some coffee?

Exercise 8
1 f 2 d 3 a 4 b 5 c 6 e

Exercise 9
Andreas will be late.

Exercise 10
1 Hi everyone, **good to see you** all.
2 Does **everyone have** a copy of the agenda for today?
3 And **has anyone seen** Julia today?
4 She's not here today. She's not **feeling well**.

Exercise 11
1 Is Peter is on his way?
2 Has anyone seen Anna today?
3 Does everyone have the agenda?
4 Would anyone like some tea or coffee?
5 Shall we get started?

1 b 2 e 3 a 4 d 5 c

Exercises 12 + 13 (open answers)

Unit 2

Exercise 1
1 d 2 a 3 b 4 c

Exercise 2
It's a kick-off meeting
Yes, the participants all work in the same company.

Exercise 3
1 I've **been with** the company for about ten years …
2 I moved here from our office in the States **two years ago**.
3 I've worked **on similar projects** for other departments …
4 **I just moved** here from another company …
5 I **work in** the finance department and …
6 … I'll be **in charge of** the budget…
7 I still **work closely** with the team there …
8 I work in the IT department and **will be responsible** for the team who will do the programming.
9 **I'm head of** customer relations …
10 I'm **part of the** research and development department …
11 … and I'm **leading** this project.

Exercise 4
1 with 2 in 3 on 4 with, for 5 of 6 to

Exercise 5
1 d 2 b 3 f 4 c 5 a 6 e

Exercise 6
1 T
2 T
3 F – It takes place in the afternoon.
4 F – He is late.

Exercise 7
(model answers)
1 It takes place on Thursday, June 4, 20.. from 3:00 to 4:15 p.m. in the conference room (2.033).
2 Eight people are attending the meeting. / There are eight attendees (or participants), including the special guests.
3 They are having the meeting to give updates.
4 There are six items on the agenda.

Exercise 8
1 late 2 started 3 agenda 4 items 5 updates 6 budget

Exercise 9
1 Shall we **go through the agenda** first?
2 Arne, can you **take the minutes** today?
3 The **main items on** the agenda are …
4 Are there **any other points** we should add?

Exercises 10–12 (open answers)

Unit 3

Exercise 1 (open answers)

Exercise 2
Dialogues 2 and 3

Exercise 3
1 **What's the news on** the stand for the trade fair?
2 **How is** the monthly newsletter going?
3 Can you **give me an update on** that?
4 Well, **we finished** the design concept.
5 At **the moment** we're building the stand and …
6 … everything's **on schedule**.
7 We're **still waiting for** an update from our supplier.
8 I emailed them but they **haven't answered yet**.
9 **We're visiting** some new venues this week

Exercise 4
1 Can you give us   an update on …?
2 How is   that going?
3 … it should be here   next week.
4 Everything's   on schedule.
5 We haven't found   anyone yet.
6 We've already   ordered it …
7 What's the   news …?

a 1, 2, 7   b 3, 4, 5, 6

Exercise 5
1 What's the news
2 we've already ordered it
3 it should be here next week
4 How is that going
5 We haven't found anyone yet
6 Can you give us an update on
7 Everything's on schedule

Exercise 6
On the to-do list: check technical equipment, book conference room, finish reports, print contracts
Jana delegates: check technical equipment

Exercise 7
1 Sorry, **did you say** Tuesday or Thursday?
2 So there will be 14 of us at the meeting, **right**?
3 Sorry, **was that** 218 or 219?
4 **Do you mean** six copies of the whole contract?
5 I **can do that**, no problem.
6 Yes, I'll **take care of** that.
7 **Fine**, just the first five pages then.
8 I'll **do that right away**.

Exercise 8
1 mean 2 right away 3 Actually 4 take care 5 was
6 right 7 afraid 8 by

Exercise 9
(model answers)
1 Sorry, was that the 5th or the 25th (of June)?
  Did you say seven or eight copies?
2 Sorry, who should I call? / Sorry, who do you want me to call?
  Do you mean this Friday or next Friday? / Was that this Friday or next Friday?
3 Do you mean the conference on May 6th or 16th? / Which conference do you mean?
  Was that the conference on May 6th or 16th?
4 Sorry, I'm afraid I have no time right now / at the moment.

Exercises 10–12 (open answers)

Unit 4

Exercise 1 (open answer)

Exercise 2
Janina thinks it is a good idea to start the launch later.

Exercise 3
1 put half the parking under the building
2 do the construction work in the summer

Exercise 4
1 In **my opinion**, March is a little early.
2 In **my experience**, delays are quite common.
3 I **don't think** that will be a problem.
4 Sure, that **sounds like** a good idea.
5 Yes, **I think so** too.
6 Yes, **I agree.** It will reduce costs …
7 Personally, I **think we should** move the launch to June.
8 **What about putting** half the parking under the building?

Exercise 5
1 e 2 f 3 c 4 b 5 d 6 a

Exercise 6
1 In my opinion
2 Why don't we check
3 I think we have
4 What about speaking

a 3 b 1 c 2 d 4

Exercise 7
Julia disagrees with Stuart

Exercise 8
1 **Actually**, I think it's important
2 I see **your point**, Stuart, but …
3 Well, I'm afraid I **don't agree**.

Exercise 9
1 don't agree 2 point 3 agree 4 Actually

Exercise 10
agree: Lisa, Jürgen, Beate
disagree: Dan, Raul

1 completely, I think
2 Sorry
3 I see Jürgen's point
4 What about, Actually

Exercises 11–13 (open answers)

Answer key 57

Unit 5

Exercise 1 (open answers)

Exercise 2
Missing a deadline

Exercise 3
1 Sales of bestseller
2 Selling online
3 Summer special offer

Exercise 4
1 I'm afraid **we don't have enough** parts left in the warehouse …
2 We **have a problem**. Sales of our best-selling product are going down.
3 **Unfortunately**, there's a new product on the market …
4 OK, so **what can** we do?
5 What **do you think**, Werner?
6 Any **other ideas**?
7 Would it **be possible** to move the deadline?
8 What do you think? Would **that work**?
9 We **could** sell it online?
10 I'll **see what information** I can find about online retailers.

Exercise 5
1 b 2 e 3 c 4 a 5 f 6 d

Exercise 6
1 I'm afraid
2 What can we do?
3 we have a problem
4 I'll look into

Exercise 7
1 f 2 d 3 b 4 a 5 c 6 e

Exercise 8
1 presentation 2 report 3 stand 4 personnel

Exercise 9
1 Can I **get back to you** on Wednesday?
2 Could we **look at it** tomorrow?
3 Could we **wait until we hear back** from the organizers about prices?
4 I'm afraid we don't have enough time. – That's OK. **Let's talk about them** next week.

Exercise 10
(model answers)
1 Could we discuss this later? We don't have enough time now.
2 Sorry, I'm afraid I don't have enough time to finish this now. Let's talk about it tomorrow.
3 Sorry, can we wait until I hear back from the team in the States? They haven't contacted me yet.
4 Can I get back to you on that? I'm still waiting for the sales figures.

Exercises 11 + 12 (open answers)

Unit 6

Exercise 1
1 L 2 B 3 B 4 B 5 B 6 L

Exercise 2
They follow the advice.
The participants talk about the weather. Other good small-talk topics are sports or vacations/travel.

Exercise 3
c Nadja's connection is bad.

Exercise 4
1 Can **everyone hear** me OK?
2 Hello Florian, **this is** John.
3 Has Julien **logged in** yet?
4 Is **the line** OK?
5 No, **sorry, I can't hear you**.
6 There's a problem **with my line**.
7 Could you **repeat that**, please?
8 I'll **hang up and dial in** again.
9 Nadja here. Does that **sound better**?

Exercise 5
1 c 2 d 3 e 4 b 5 a

Exercise 6
1 in, for 2 up 3 about 4 up, in

Exercise 7
1 Anika 2 Peter 3 Ralf 4 Tara

Exercise 8
1 Sorry, **who's** speaking?
2 Ralf, did you want to **add anything** to that?
3 Excuse me, this is Ralf. **What do you mean by** "downsides"?
4 Sorry, I **didn't get the** last part.
5 **In other words**, you think we should stay with our current supplier.
6 But, **just to be clear**, only the details for the two suppliers …

Exercise 9
1 who's speaking 2 Excuse me 3 Just to be clear
4 Do you mean 5 I didn't get 6 In other words

Exercise 10
1 f 2 d 3 e 4 c 5 a 6 b

Exercises 11 + 12 (open answers)

Unit 7

Exercise 1 (open answers)

Exercise 2
They are meeting on Friday at 2:15 for a strategy meeting.

Exercise 3
1 T
2 F – She talked to the HR department, but she doesn't work there.
3 F – It's planned for Tuesday.
4 F – It will take place in the TRS office in Bremen.

Exercise 4

1 So, **could we** meet on Thursday?
2 I'm afraid **I can't make** Thursday.
3 **How about** Friday afternoon at 2:00?
4 That's fine, but I **might be** a few minutes late.
5 Why **don't we say** 2:15 then?
6 We **would like to set up** a meeting on Tuesday, October 25 …
7 Could you **let me know by** Friday if that would work for you?
8 Please **get in touch** if you have any questions.
9 I look forward **to seeing you** again soon.

Exercise 5

1 Would it be possible to — meet on Wednesday afternoon instead?
2 Could you let us know — by Friday at the latest?
3 I look forward to — seeing you on Friday.
4 Could we set up — a meeting next Tuesday in my office?
5 Would 9:00 or 9:30 — work better for you?
6 Why don't we say — 3:00 p.m. then?

a 3 b 2 c 4 d 1 e 6 f 5

Exercise 6

1 Thanks for (not ~~thanks~~ for) 2 set up a meeting 3 let me know 4 get in touch 5 look forward 6 Best wishes (not ~~best~~ wishes)

Exercise 7

1 c 2 b 3 d 4 a

(model answer)
The email to Rasmus is less formal than the email to Petra. Mike writes "Hi", not "Dear", and he also starts the email with some small talk (I hope you had a good weekend.). In the email to Rasmus, he uses shorter sentences ("Let me know!", not "Could you let me know if you can make it?") and an exclamation mark (!).

Exercise 8

	Why do they need to rearrange their meeting?	When are they planning to meet now?
1	Theo has an urgent appointment with a client.	Tuesday at 9:00 a.m.
2	John cancelled the appointment because he is not feeling well.	Monday at 2:00 p.m.

Exercise 9

1 I **have to cancel** our meeting this afternoon.
2 **Can we meet at** another time then?
3 Sorry, but Monday **doesn't work** for me.
4 Tuesday morning. Let me see. Yes, I **should be free** then.
5 **So that's** Tuesday at 9:00 a.m. Great.
6 I just **want to confirm** that I can make Monday at 2:00.

Exercise 10

1 make 2 appointment 3 meet 4 How 5 should 6 that's 7 then

Exercises 11–13 (open answers)

Unit 8

Exercise 1

1 M, E 2 E 3 B 4 B 5 E 6 B 7 M, E 8 B 9 E
10 B, M, E

Exercise 2

Tasks 3, 4, 6, 8

2 Proposal 4 Next milestones

Exercise 3

1 So, **we're here today** to talk about strategy for AISCO.
2 The **first item on the agenda** is a progress report from Adam.
3 Then **we'll move on to** the proposal.
4 And **finally, we'll talk about** the next milestones.

Exercise 4

1 We're here today to talk about …
2 The first item on the agenda is …
3 Then we'll move on to …
4 After that we will look at …
5 Finally, we'll talk about …

Exercise 5 (open answers)

Exercise 6

b They don't have enough time.

Andrew does tasks 2, 5, 7, 9 and 10.

Exercise 7

1 Does everyone **agree with** them?
2 What does **everyone else** think?
3 Unfortunately, we don't have **much time left**.
4 So, that's all we **have time for**.
5 So, **to summarize**, today we talked about …
6 And Adam, you're **responsible for** next week's agenda.

Exercise 8

1 think we should
2 agree with that
3 have time for
4 put it on
5 quickly summarize
6 can finish there
7 the minutes from
8 for coming

Exercise 9

(model answers)
1 Does everyone agree with the suggestion?
2 What do you think, Maria? And you, John?
3 Can you please finish your point? Unfortunately, we don't have much time left.
4 So, to summarize, today we talked about …
5 Could you prepare next week's agenda, please?
6 Thanks for coming, everyone. See you next time!

Exercises 10–12 (open answers)

Key phrases

Getting started

Greeting someone you don't know	**Jemand Unbekanntes grüßen**
You must be Ms. Kowalski.	Sie sind bestimmt Frau Kowalski.
It's a pleasure to (finally) meet you.	Es ist eine Freude, Sie (endlich) kennenzulernen.
It's nice to meet you (too).	(Ebenfalls) Schön, Sie kennenzulernen.
Pleased to meet you.	Freut mich, Sie kennenzulernen.
I look forward to working with you.	Ich freue mich darauf, mit Ihnen zusammenzuarbeiten.

Introducing yourself	**Sich vorstellen**
I'm Anna Schmidt, but please call me Anna. – And I'm David.	Ich bin Anna Schmidt, aber sagen Sie ruhig Anna zu mir. – Und ich bin David.
I don't think we've met. My name is Jan Golz.	Ich glaube, wir kennen uns noch nicht. Mein Name ist Jan Golz.

Greeting someone you know	**Jemand Bekanntes begrüßen**
It's nice / Nice to see you (again). – Good to see you too.	Schön Sie wiederzusehen. – Ich freue mich auch.
How are you? – I'm well. / Not bad, thanks.	Wie geht es Ihnen? – Es geht mir gut. / Nicht schlecht, danke.
How are things? – Good, thanks. And with you?	Wie läuft es? – Gut, danke. Und bei Ihnen?

Introducing someone	**Jemanden vorstellen**
I'd like to introduce a new colleague. She's responsible for …	Ich möchte gerne eine neue Kollegin vorstellen. Sie ist zuständig für …
This is my colleague Maria Lopez.	Das ist meine Kollegin Maria Lopez.
I don't think you've met.	Ich glaube, Sie kennen sich noch nicht.

Making someone welcome	**Jemanden willkommen heißen**
Can I take your coat? – Thank you.	Kann ich Ihnen Ihren Mantel abnehmen? – Danke.
Please take a seat and have some coffee/tea/water if you'd like.	Setzen Sie sich und nehmen Sie sich bitte etwas Kaffee/Tee/Wasser.
Would you like some coffee?	Möchten Sie einen Kaffee?

Making small talk

Is this your first time in Frankfurt?
- No, I was here last year, so I know the city a little.
- Yes, it is. But I've wanted to come for a while.

Did you find us OK?
- Yes, thank you.

How was your flight / trip / train ride?
- Fine, thanks.

Talking about participants

Is Andreas on his way?
- Yes, he'll be here in a minute.

And has anyone seen Julia?
- She's not here today. She's not feeling well.

Starting a meeting

Well, shall we start?
So, let's get started.
So, I think we should get started.
Good morning / Good afternoon / Hi (everyone).
It's good to see you all.
Thank you (all) for coming.
Did everyone get / Does everyone have a copy of the agenda?

Small Talk führen

Sind Sie zum ersten Mal in Frankfurt?
- Nein, ich war schon letztes Jahr hier und kenne die Stadt also ein bisschen.
- Ja, ist es, aber ich wollte schon länger mal herkommen.

Haben Sie gut hergefunden?
- Ja, danke.

Wie war Ihr/e Flug/Reise/Zugfahrt?
- Gut, danke.

Über Teilnehmer sprechen

Ist Andreas auf dem Weg?
- Ja, er wird gleich hier sein.

Hat jemand Julia gesehen?
- Sie ist heute nicht hier. Es geht ihr nicht gut.

Ein Meeting eröffnen

Sollen wir anfangen?
So, fangen wir an.
Ich denke, wir sollten anfangen.
Guten Morgen / Guten Tag / Hallo (allerseits).
Schön, dass Sie alle da sind.
Danke, dass Sie (alle) gekommen sind.
Hat jeder eine Kopie der Tagesordnung (bekommen)?

Beginning the meeting

Describing your job or role

I work in the … department and I'll be in charge of …
I work closely with the team here / there / in Poland.
I'm head of …
I'm part of the … department.
I am / will be responsible for …

I'm leading this project.

Die eigene Arbeit oder Rolle beschreiben

Ich arbeite in der Abteilung … und werde für … zuständig sein.
Ich arbeite eng mit dem Team hier / dort / in Polen zusammen.
Ich bin Leiter/in von …
Ich bin Teil der …abteilung.
Ich bin zuständig für … / werde für … zuständig sein.
Ich leite dieses Projekt.

Departments	Abteilungen
accounting	Buchhaltung
customer relations	Kundenbetreuung
finance	Finanzabteilung
HR (human resources)	Personalabteilung
IT (information technology)	IT
marketing	Marketing
production	Herstellung
purchasing	Einkauf
quality control	Qualitätsmanagement
R&D (research and development)	F&E (Forschung und Entwicklung)
sales	Vertrieb, Verkauf

Talking about your experience	Eigene Erfahrung schildern
I've been with the company for about ten years.	Ich arbeite seit ungefähr 10 Jahren für diese Firma.
I moved here from our Chicago office (two years ago).	Ich bin (vor zwei Jahren) von unserem Sitz in Chicago hergezogen.
I just moved here from production / another company.	Ich bin gerade von der Herstellung / einer anderen Firma hierher gewechselt.
I've worked on similar projects for other departments.	Ich habe für andere Abteilungen an ähnlichen Projekten gearbeitet.

Talking about the agenda	Über die Tagesordnung sprechen
Did everyone get / Does everyone have a copy of the agenda?	Hat jeder eine Kopie der Tagesordnung (bekommen)?
Here is a copy of the agenda.	Hier ist eine Kopie der Tagesordnung.
Shall we go through the agenda first?	Sollen wir uns zuerst die Tagesordnung anschauen?
The main items on the agenda are …	Die Hauptpunkte der Tagesordnung sind …
Are there any other points we should add?	Gibt es noch weitere Punkte, die wir zufügen sollten?
Can you take the minutes today?	Schreiben Sie heute das Protokoll?

Types of meetings	Meetingsarten
one-on-one meeting	Persönliches Gespräch
departmental meeting	Abteilungsmeeting
kick-off meeting	Kick-off Meeting
teleconference (meeting)	Telekonferenz
regular/weekly meeting	reguläres/wöchentliches Meeting, Jour Fixe

Giving updates

Asking for an update
What's the news on …?
Is there any news on …?
How is the project going?
Can you give me/us an update?

How are you doing with …?

Ein Update einfordern
Was gibt es Neues bei …?
Gibt es Neuigkeiten über …?
Wie läuft das Projekt?
Können Sie mich/uns auf den neuesten Stand bringen?
Wie läuft es bei Ihnen mit …?

Giving an update
We finished the …
We've already ordered/done …
We haven't done … yet.
We're still waiting for …
We're visiting some new venues this week.

At the moment, we're building/visiting …
We're on schedule.
We'll meet the deadline.

Ein Update geben
Wir haben … abgeschlossen.
Wir haben … schon bestellt/erledigt.
Wir haben … noch nicht erledigt.
Wir warten noch auf …
Wir besuchen diese Woche ein paar neue Tagungsorte.
Zurzeit bauen/besuchen wir …
Wir liegen im Zeitplan.
Wir werden die Frist einhalten.

Checking understanding
Sorry, was that … or …?
Sorry, but did you say Tuesday or Thursday?

So there will be …, right?
Do you mean …?

Rückfragen stellen
Entschuldigung, war das … oder …?
Entschuldigung, aber sagten Sie Dienstag oder Donnerstag?
Es wird also … geben, richtig?
Meinen Sie …?

Accepting tasks (or not)
I can do that, no problem.
Fine. I'll do it/that right away.
I can / I'll take care of that.
Sorry, I'm afraid I can't right now.

Aufgaben (nicht) annehmen
Das kann ich machen, kein Problem.
In Ordnung. Ich erledige es/das sofort.
Ich kann/werde mich darum kümmern.
Tut mir leid, im Moment kann ich nicht.

Taking part in a discussion

Giving your opinion
In my opinion, …
In my experience, …
Personally, I think …
I don't think that's a problem.
It's important to …

Die eigene Meinung wiedergeben
Meiner Meinung nach …
Meiner Erfahrung nach …
Ich persönlich denke …
Ich denke nicht, dass das ein Problem ist.
Es ist wichtig, dass …

Making a suggestion	**Einen Vorschlag machen**
I think we should …	Ich denke, wir sollten …
We could …	Wir könnten …
Let's change …	Ändern wir …
How/What about doing …?	Wie wäre es, wenn wir … machen?
Why don't we …?	Warum machen wir nicht folgendes …?

Agreeing	**Zustimmen**
That sounds like a good idea.	Das klingt nach einer guten Idee.
Yes, I think so too.	Ja, das denke ich auch.
Yes, I agree (with Phil).	Ja, ich stimme (Phil) zu.

Disagreeing	**Widersprechen**
I don't agree.	Ich stimme nicht zu.
I'm afraid I don't agree.	Ich stimme leider nicht zu.
Actually, …	Eigentlich …
Yes, but …	Ja, aber …
I see your point, but …	Ich verstehe Ihr Argument, aber …

Problems and solutions

Describing a problem	**Ein Problem beschreiben**
We have a problem.	Wir haben ein Problem.
I'm afraid …	Leider …
Unfortunately, …	Bedauerlicherweise …
Sorry, but it looks like …	Tut mir leid, aber es sieht so aus, als ob …

Looking for a solution	**Nach einer Lösung suchen**
OK, so what can/could we do?	OK, also was können/könnten wir tun?
What do you think?	Was denken Sie?
Any other ideas?	Gibt es weitere Ideen?

Offering a solution	**Eine Lösung anbieten**
Would it be possible to …?	Wäre es möglich, …?
Well, we have to think about …	Wir müssen über … nachdenken.
We could …	Wir könnten …
How about …?	Wie wäre es mit …?
Would that work?	Würde das funktionieren?
I'll see what information I can find.	Mal schauen, welche Informationen ich finden kann.
I'll look into that.	Ich prüfe das.

Delaying making a decision	**Eine Entscheidung hinauszögern**
Can I get back to you on Wednesday?	Kann ich mich am Mittwoch nochmal melden?
Could we look at it again next week?	Können wir uns das nächste Woche nochmal anschauen?
It's difficult to say right now …	Das ist jetzt schwer zu sagen …
Can we wait until …?	Können wir bis … warten?
Let's talk about … tomorrow/later.	Lassen Sie uns über … morgen/später sprechen.

Conference calls

Entering a call and getting started	**In eine Telekonferenz beitreten und anfangen**
Can everyone hear me OK?	Versteht mich jeder?
Hello Florian, this is John.	Hallo Florian, hier spricht John.
Hi Florian, Nadja here.	Hi Florian, hier ist Nadja.
Is everyone logged in?	Ist jeder eingeloggt?
Are we all ready to begin?	Sind wir alle bereit anzufangen?
Is the line OK?	Ist die Verbindung gut?
Shall we get started then?	Können wir anfangen?

Dealing with problems	**Mit Problemen umgehen**
Sorry, I can't hear you. Can you say that again?	Tut mir leid, ich kann Sie nicht hören. Können Sie das wiederholen?
Could you repeat that, please?	Können Sie das bitte wiederholen?
Could you turn up the volume, please?	Können Sie bitte etwas lauter machen?
Wait a minute. There's a problem with my line.	Warten Sie kurz. Ich habe ein Problem mit meiner Verbindung.
I'll hang up and dial in again.	Ich lege auf und rufe nochmal an.
One moment, let me try and call again.	Einen Moment, ich versuche, nochmal anzurufen.
Does that sound better?	Klingt es jetzt besser?
That's a lot clearer.	Es ist viel deutlicher.

Clarifying information	**Informationen klären**
Sorry, who's speaking?	Entschuldigung, wer spricht da?
Did you want to add anything to that?	Wollen Sie noch etwas hinzufügen?
Excuse me. What do you mean by …?	Entschuldigung, aber was meinen Sie mit …?
Sorry, I didn't get that / the last part.	Entschuldigung, das / den letzten Teil habe ich nicht verstanden.
Do you mean we should …?	Meinen Sie, dass wir … sollten?
In other words, …	Anders formuliert, …
Just to be clear, …	Nur um sicherzugehen, …

Arranging a meeting

Arranging a meeting	**Eine Besprechung organisieren**
Could/Can we meet on Friday morning at 9:00?	Könnten/Können wir uns Freitagmorgen um 9:00 treffen?
How about Monday at 3:00 p.m.?	Wie wäre es mit Montag um 15:00 Uhr?
What about Tuesday morning?	Wie wäre es mit Dienstagmorgen?
Why don't we say 2:15 then?	Dann lassen Sie uns 14:15 abmachen.

Arranging a meeting by email (formal/neutral)	**Eine Besprechung per Email organisieren (formell/neutral)**
We would like to set up a meeting on Tuesday, October 25.	Wir würden gerne ein Meeting für Dienstag, den 25. Oktober, ansetzen.
Could you let me know by Friday if that would work for you / if you can make it?	Können Sie mich bitte bis Freitag wissen lassen, ob es Ihnen passt / ob Sie es schaffen?
Would Wednesday at 11:00 be OK for you?	Passt Ihnen Mittwoch um 11:00 Uhr?
Please get in touch if you have any questions.	Bitte melden Sie sich, falls Sie irgendwelche Fragen haben.
I look forward to seeing you (again soon).	Ich freue mich darauf, Sie (bald wieder) zu sehen.

Arranging a meeting by email (informal)	**Eine Besprechung per E-Mail organisieren (informell)**
Can we meet Thursday at 10:30 to work on …?	Können wir uns am Donnerstag um 10:30 treffen, um an … zu arbeiten?
Let me know (if you can make it).	Sagen Sie Bescheid, (ob Sie es schaffen).

Saying you can or can't attend	**Sagen, dass man (nicht) teilnehmen kann**
Thursday morning after 10:00 a.m. would work (for me).	Donnerstagmorgen nach 10:00 Uhr wäre (für mich) in Ordnung.
Tuesday sounds good.	Dienstag klingt gut.
I'm afraid I can't make Friday.	Am Freitag kann ich leider nicht.
Sorry, I can't make 2:00 p.m.	Tut mir leid, 14:00 Uhr schaffe ich nicht.
Sorry, but Monday doesn't work for me.	Tut mir leid, aber am Montag kann ich nicht.

Rearranging a meeting	**Eine Besprechung verschieben**
I'm really sorry. I have to cancel our meeting this afternoon.	Es tut mir sehr leid, aber ich muss unser Meeting heute Nachtmittag absagen.
I have an urgent appointment.	Ich habe einen wichtigen Termin.
Unfortunately, I can't come to the meeting today / tomorrow / next week.	Leider kann ich an dem Meeting heute / morgen / nächste Woche nicht teilnehmen.
Can you make it on another day?	Passt es Ihnen an einem anderen Tag?
Would it be possible to meet on/at … instead?	Ist es möglich, sich stattdessen am/um … zu treffen?
Let me see. Yes, I should be free then.	Ich schaue mal nach. Ja, da habe ich Zeit.

Confirming a meeting	**Ein Meeting bestätigen**
So that's Tuesday at 9:00 a.m. Great.	Also am Dienstag um 9:00 Uhr. Sehr gut.
I'll send you an email to confirm.	Ich werde eine Bestätigungsemail schicken.
I just want to confirm that I can make Monday at 2:00.	Ich möchte nur gerade bestätigen, dass ich am Montag 14:00 Uhr kommen werde.

Leading a meeting

Introducing the agenda | Die Tagesordnung einbringen

So, we're here today to talk about …	Wir wollen heute über … sprechen.
The first item on the agenda is …	Der erste Punkt auf der Tagesordnung ist …
We'll start with …	Fangen wir mit … an.
Then, we'll move on to …	Dann gehen wir über zu …
After that, we will look at …	Danach schauen wir uns … an.
And finally, we'll talk about …	Abschließend sprechen wir über …

Asking for feedback | Um Stellungnahme bitten

Does everyone agree with the milestones / the decision?	Stimmt jeder diesen Meilensteinen / dieser Entscheidung zu?
Mary, do you agree?	Mary, stimmen Sie zu?
What do you think, John?	Was denken Sie, John?
What does everyone else think?	Was ist die Meinung der anderen hierzu?

Checking the time | Die Uhr im Auge behalten

Can I stop you there?	Kann ich Sie da mal unterbrechen?
Unfortunately, we don't have much time left.	Leider haben wir nicht mehr viel Zeit.
Let's put that on next week's agenda.	Setzen wir es auf die Tagesordnung für nächste Woche.
So, that's all we have time for today.	Für mehr haben wir heute keine Zeit.

Delegating tasks | Aufgaben delegieren

Can you send everyone the minutes from today?	Können Sie jedem das Protokoll von heute schicken?
Kerstin will send me information about …, and Adam will follow up on …	Kerstin schickt mir die Information bezüglich … und Adam bearbeitet … weiter.
Adam, you're responsible for …	Adam, Sie sind zuständig für …

Summarizing and closing a meeting | Ein Meeting zusammenfassen und beenden

So, that's all we have time for today.	Für mehr haben wir heute keine Zeit.
I think we should stop / can finish there.	Ich denke, an dieser Stelle sollten/können wir aufhören.
Let me just (quickly) summarize what we discussed today.	Lassen Sie mich gerade (schnell) zusammenfassen, worüber wir heute gesprochen haben.
So, to summarize, today we talked about …	Um also zusammenzufassen, wir haben heute über … gesprochen.
Thanks for coming. See you next time/week.	Danke, dass Sie da waren. Bis nächste Woche. / Bis zum nächsten Mal.

A–Z wordlist

A
able, to be ~ to	fähig sein, im Stande sein
to accept	akzeptieren, annehmen
accounting	Buchhaltung
action point	Maßnahme, Aktion
actually	eigentlich
to add	hinzufügen
to advertise	werben, Werbung machen
advice	Rat, Ratschlag, Ratschläge
afraid, I'm ~ (that)	leider
agency	Agentur
agenda	Tagesordnung
to agree to sth.	sich auf etw. einigen
to agree with sb.	gleicher Meinung wie jd. sein, jdm. zustimmen
to agree with sth.	mit etw. übereinstimmen
already	schon, bereits
another	andere/r/s, weitere/r/s
apology	Entschuldigung
appointment	Termin
to arrange	(Termin usw.) ausmachen, vereinbaren, arrangieren
to arrive	eintreffen, ankommen
asleep, to fall ~	einschlafen
assistant	Assistent/in
to attend sth.	an etw. teilnehmen
attendee	Teilnehmer/in
attitude	Einstellung, Haltung
away	weg, abwesend

B
back, to get ~ to sb.	sich wieder bei jdm. melden, jdm. antworten
back, to hear ~ from sb.	eine Antwort von jdm. bekommen, von jdm. hören
bad, That's too ~.	Schade.
because	weil, denn
to begin	beginnen, anfangen
beginning	Anfang
below	unten (stehend)
bill	Rechnung
body language	Körpersprache
to book	buchen, reservieren
both	beide
budget	Budget, Etat
budget, to go over ~	ein Budget überschreiten
budget plan	Finanzplan, Kostenplan
to build	bauen, aufbauen

C
calendar	Kalender
call	Anruf
to call	nennen, rufen; anrufen
to cancel	stornieren, streichen, absagen
capital letter	Großbuchstabe
care, to take ~ of sb./sth.	sich um jdn./etw. kümmern
to chair	(Sitzung) leiten
chairperson	Vorsitzende/r
challenge	Herausforderung, (schwierige) Aufgabe
chance	Gelegenheit
change	Veränderung, Wechsel, Wandel; Änderung
to change	wechseln, tauschen; ändern
charge, to be in ~ of sth.	für etw. zuständig sein, für etw. verantwortlich sein
chat	(lockeres) Gespräch
to chat	reden, quatschen
cheap	günstig, billig
to check	überprüfen, kontrollieren
to clarify	klarstellen, klären
client	Kunde/Kundin
close(ly)	eng
coat	Mantel, Jacke
colleague	Kollege/Kollegin
comment	Kommentar, Stellungnahme
common	gängig, üblich, häufig, verbreitet
to compare	vergleichen
to complete	vervollständigen
conference call	Telefonkonferenz, Konferenzschaltung
to confirm	bestätigen, (Termin) zusagen
connection	Verbindung
consultant	Berater/in
to contact sb.	sich mit jdm. in Verbindung setzen
to continue	fortfahren, weitermachen; weitergehen
contract	Vertrag
conversation	Gespräch, Unterhaltung
copy	Exemplar
costs, to reduce ~	Kosten senken
course, of ~	natürlich, selbstverständlich
culture	Kultur
current(ly)	aktuell, gegenwärtig
customer relations	Kundendienst

D
deadline	Frist, Termin
deadline, to meet a ~	eine Frist einhalten
deal	(günstiges) Geschäft, Angebot
to deal with sth.	mit etw. umgehen, mit etw. zu tun haben
to decide	entscheiden, beschließen; festlegen
decision	Entscheidung
decision-making	Entscheidungsfindung
delay	Verzögerung, Verspätung
to delay	verzögern, aufhalten; aufschieben
to delegate sth. to sb.	etw. an jdn. delegieren
to deliver	liefern
delivery	Lieferung

department	Abteilung
departmental	Abteilungs-
to describe	beschreiben
design	Entwurf, Design
details	Angaben, Details
to dial in	(Telefon:) sich einwählen
different	verschieden, unterschiedlich
difficult	schwierig, schwer
to disagree with sb.	jdm. nicht zustimmen, anderer Meinung als jd. sein
to disagree with sth.	einer Sache nicht zustimmen
discount	Rabatt
to discuss sth.	über etw. sprechen, etw. diskutieren
discussion	Gespräch, Diskussion
disorganized	planlos, unorganisiert
documents pl	Unterlagen
downside	Nachteil

E

e.g.	z. B.
early	früh
easy	leicht, einfach
to email sb.	jdm. eine E-Mail schicken
embarrassing	peinlich
enough	genügend, genug
to enter sth.	etw. (Passwort usw.) eingeben; zu etw. (Gespräch usw.) dazukommen
equipment	Geräte, Ausstattung
especially	besonders, insbesondere
excellent	ausgezeichnet
expensive	teuer
experience	Erfahrung(en), Erlebnis(se)
to experience sth.	etw. erleben
to explain	erklären, erläutern
extra	zusätzlich

F

face to face	persönlich
factory	Fabrik, Werk
fair, trade ~	Messe, Fachmesse
to fall asleep	einschlafen
false	falsch
familiar	vertraut
feedback	Reaktionen, Meinungen
to feel	(sich) fühlen
figures	Zahlen
finally	endlich; schließlich, zuletzt, abschließend
finance department	Finanzabteilung
fine	gut, prima
to finish	fertig sein; beenden
firm	Firma
first name	Vorname
fixed	fest, festgelegt
flexible	anpassungsfähig, flexibel
flight	Flug
to fly by	vorüberfliegen
to focus on sth.	sich auf etw. konzentrieren
to follow	folgen, befolgen
to follow up on sth.	einer Sache nachgehen, etw. nachverfolgen
following, the ~	das Folgende, folgendes
follow-up	Folge-, nachfolgend
to forget	vergessen
formal	förmlich, formell
forward, to look ~ to sth.	sich auf etw. freuen
free, to be ~	Zeit haben
furniture	Möbel

G

to get back to sb.	sich wieder bei jdm. melden, jdm. antworten
to get in touch	sich melden;
to get started	anfangen, loslegen
to get to know sb.	jdn. kennenlernen
to go wrong	schieflaufen
to greet sb.	jdn. begrüßen
greeting	Begrüßung
to guess	meinen, glauben
guest	Gast

H

to hang up	(Telefon:) auflegen
happy, to be ~ to do sth.	gern bereit sein, etw. zu tun
head	(Abteilungs-)Leiter/in
to hear back from sb.	eine Antwort von jdm. bekommen, von jdm. hören
to hold (the line)	am Telefon bleiben
honest	ehrlich
to hope	hoffen
human resources (HR)	Personalabteilung

I

importance	Bedeutung, Wichtigkeit
important	wichtig, bedeutend
impressed	beeindruckt
to improve	verbessern
to include sb.	jdn. einbeziehen
information	Angaben, Information(en)
instead	stattdessen
to introduce sb./sth. to sb.	jdn./etw. jdm. vorstellen
introduction	Vorstellung
invitation	Einladung
to invite sb.	jdn. einladen
invoice	Rechnung
issue	Problem
item	(Tagesordnungs-)Punkt

J K

to join	(neu) hinzukommen
to keep to sth.	sich an etw. halten
key	Schlüssel(-), wichtig; Taste
kick-off	Auftakt, Start
to know	wissen; kennen
know, to get to ~ sb.	jdn. kennenlernen
know, to let sb. ~	jdm. Bescheid geben/sagen

L

last but not least	zu guter Letzt
late	(zu) spät
latest, at the ~	spätestens
launch	Markteinführung
to lead	leiten, führen
to leave a message	eine Nachricht hinterlassen

lesson, to learn a ~	etw. daraus lernen	**P**	
to let sb. know	jdm. Bescheid geben/sagen	packaging	Verpackung
level	Niveau	parking	Parkplätze
line	Leitung, (Telefon-)Verbindung	part	Teil; Bauteil, Ersatzteil
		part, to take ~ in sth.	an etw. teilnehmen
little, a ~	ein wenig	participant	Teilnehmer/in
to log in	sich einloggen	personal(ly)	persönlich
to look forward to sth.	sich auf etw. freuen	personnel	Personal
to look into sth.	sich um etw. kümmern	place, to take ~	stattfinden
look, to have a ~ at sth.	sich etw. ansehen	policy	Strategie, Regeln, Politik
low	niedrig	polite(ly)	höflich
		pound key	Rautetaste
M		to prefer	vorziehen
main	Haupt-; wichtigste/r/s	preparation	Vorbereitung
to make it/sth.	es/etw. schaffen	to prepare	(sich) vorbereiten
to make sure	dafür sorgen, sicherstellen	to present sth.	etw. vorstellen, etw. präsentieren
market	Markt		
to mean	bedeuten; meinen	previous	vorig, vorangegangen
meaning	Bedeutung	price	Preis
meantime, in the ~	in der Zwischenzeit	to print (out)	(aus)drucken
to meet	begegnen, kennenlernen, treffen	production	Herstellung, Produktion
		programming	Programmieren, Programmierung
to meet a deadline	eine Frist einhalten		
member	Mitglied	progress	Fortschritt(e), Verlauf
message	Nachricht, Mitteilung	progress report	Zwischenbericht
message, text ~	SMS	prompt	Stichwort, Aufforderung
middle	Mitte	proposal	Vorschlag, Angebot
milestone	Projektabschnitt, Meilenstein	purchasing	Einkauf
minute, in a ~	gleich, jeden Moment	**Q R**	
minutes, to take the ~	Protokoll führen	quality control	Qualitätskontrolle
miscellaneous (misc.) AE	(Tagesordnung:) Sonstiges	quick(ly)	schnell
to miss sth.	etw. verpassen	quiet	ruhig, still
mistake	Fehler	to reach	erreichen
monthly	monatlich	ready (for sth.)	(für etw.) bereit
to move	umziehen	to rearrange	(Termin) verschieben
to move sth.	etw. (Termin usw.) verschieben	reason	Grund, Motiv
		to receive	erhalten, bekommen
to move on to sth.	zu etw. übergehen	recently	in letzter Zeit, neulich
movement	Bewegung	to reduce costs	Kosten senken
		regular(ly)	regelmäßig
N		relationship	Beziehung
native speaker	Muttersprachler/in	relevant to sth.	relevant/wichtig für etw.
to need	brauchen, benötigen	to repeat	wiederholen
news	Neuigkeiten, Nachrichten	to reply	antworten
normally	normalerweise, gewöhnlich	report	Bericht
now and then	ab und zu	report, progress ~	Zwischenbericht
		representative	Vertreter/in, Repräsentant/in
O			
of course	natürlich	research and development (R&D)	Forschung und Entwicklung
offer	Angebot		
offer, special ~	Sonderangebot	reservation	Reservierung
to offer sth.	etw. anbieten	responsible, to be ~ for sth.	für etw. zuständig/ verantwortlich sein
once	einmal		
one-on-one	persönlich, unter vier Augen	retailer	(Einzel-)Händler/in
		to rethink sth.	etw. überdenken
opening	Eröffnung, Beginn	to return sth.	etw. zurückgeben/-schicken
opinion	Meinung		
opinion, to give one's ~	seine Meinung wiedergeben	right away	sofort
		role	Rolle
order	Auftrag, Bestellung		
to organize	organisieren		
organizer	Organisator/in		

S

sales	Verkauf, Vertrieb; Umsatz, Verkäufe
sample	Probestück, Muster
schedule	Zeitplan
schedule, to be on ~	im Zeitplan liegen
search (for sb./sth.)	Suche (nach jdm./etw.)
seat, to take/have a ~	Platz nehmen
self-starter	jd. mit Eigeninitiative
to sell	verkaufen
to send sth. out	etw. verschicken
to set up	arrangieren, einrichten
shall	sollen
shipment	Lieferung, Versand
short, to keep sth. ~	etw. kurz halten
shy	schüchtern
similar	ähnlich, gleich
to sit down	sich setzen
slide	Präsentationsfolie
solution	Lösung
solution-oriented	lösungsorientiert
to solve	lösen
sound	Klang, Geräusch
to sound	klingen
space	Platz
special offer	Sonderangebot
to spend (on sth.)	(Geld) (für etw.) ausgeben
to spend time on sth.	sich mit etw. beschäftigen
stand	(Messe-)Stand
to start sth.	(mit) etw. beginnen/anfangen
start, to ~ with	zunächst (einmal)
started, to get ~	anfangen, loslegen
status	Stand, Status
to stay	bleiben
step	Schritt
still	(immer) noch
strategy	Strategie
stressful	stressig
structural engineer	Bauingenieur/in
structure	Struktur
stupid	albern, dumm
style	Stil
subject	Thema
successful	gelungen, erfolgreich
to suggest	vorschlagen
suggestion	Vorschlag
to summarize	zusammenfassen
supplier	Lieferant
supply	Lieferung
to supply	liefern, bereitstellen
Sure.	Natürlich./Sicherlich.
sure, to make ~	dafür sorgen, versichern
surprised	erstaunt, überrascht

T

to take part in sth.	an etw. teilnehmen
to take place	stattfinden
to take turns	sich abwechseln
task	Aufgabe
technical	technisch
teleconference	Telefonkonferenz, Konferenzschaltung
term	Begriff
text (message)	SMS
to thank	danken
though	aber, allerdings
time, for the first ~	zum ersten Mal
time, on ~	pünktlich, rechtzeitig
timeline	Zeitplan
topic	Thema
touch, to get in ~	sich melden
trade fair	Messe, Fachmesse
train ride	Zugfahrt
to travel	fahren, reisen
trip	Reise
true	wahr
to try	versuchen
to turn sth. up	etw. *(Lautstärke usw.)* hochdrehen
to turn to sth.	sich einer Sache zuwenden
turn, to be one's ~	an der Reihe sein
turn, to take ~s	sich abwechseln
twice	zweimal
type	Art
typical	typisch

U V

unfortunately	leider
update	Lagebericht, Update
to update sb.	jdn. auf den neuesten Stand bringen, jdn. über etw. informieren
urgent	dringend
to use	gebrauchen, verwenden
useful	nützlich
vacation	Urlaub, Ferien
vampire	Vampir
venue	Veranstaltungsort
to visit	besichtigen, besuchen
volume	Lautstärke

W X Y Z

to wait for sb.	auf jdn. warten
way, to be on one's ~	unterwegs sein, auf dem Weg sein
weather	Wetter
weekly	wöchentlich
welcome	willkommen
welcome, to make sb. ~	dafür sorgen, dass sich jd. wohlfühlt
to welcome sb.	jdn. begrüßen, jdn. willkommen heißen
wet	nass
whether	ob
while	während; Weile, einige Zeit
whole	ganze/r/s
whooshing sound	Rauschen, Zischen
to work	arbeiten; funktionieren
working hours	Arbeitszeiten
worldwide	auf der ganzen Welt, weltweit
to worry	sich Sorgen machen
wrong, to go ~	schieflaufen
yet, not … ~	noch nicht

Tracklist

Track	Unit	Exercise	Running time
01	Title/Copyright		0:49
02	Unit 1	Exercise 2	1:14
03	Unit 1	Exercise 3	0:48
04	Unit 1	Exercise 6	1:05
05	Unit 1	Exercise 9	0:38
06	Unit 2	Exercise 2	1:58
07	Unit 2	Exercise 6	1:11
08	Unit 2	Exercise 8	1:06
09	Unit 3	Exercise 2	1:14
10	Unit 3	Exercise 6	1:21
11	Unit 4	Exercise 2	0:48
12	Unit 4	Exercise 3	0:46
13	Unit 4	Exercise 7	1:09
14	Unit 4	Exercise 10	1:18
15	Unit 5	Exercise 2	1:05
16	Unit 5	Exercise 3	1:08
17	Unit 5	Exercise 8	1:07
18	Unit 6	Exercise 2	1:34
19	Unit 6	Exercise 3	0:55
20	Unit 6	Exercise 7	2:35
21	Unit 7	Exercise 2	0:58
22	Unit 7	Exercise 8	1:32
23	Unit 7	Exercise 10	0:33
24	Unit 8	Exercise 2	1:21
25	Unit 8	Exercise 6	1:40
26	Unit 8	Exercise 8	1:11
Total running time			31:12

Studio: Clarity Studio Berlin

Regie und Aufnahmeleitung: Christian Schmitz

Tontechnik: Christian Marx

Sprecher/innen: Tania Carlin, Malgorzata Dudley, Steve Ellery, Marianne Graffam, Melissa Holroyd, Jeffrey Mittleman, Rikke Mogensen, Lucía Palacios, Helena Prince, Justin Reddig, Dharmander Singh, Ian Smith, Tomas Sinclair Spencer, Simon Srebrny, Clare Wigfall